Travels With My Wife

Robert Downes
with Jeannette Wildman

Traverse City, Michigan
2016

The Wandering

PRESS

Published by
The Wandering Press
Traverse City, Michigan

Library of Congress Control Number: 2015903538:

ISBN 978-0-9821344-4-3

First edition published by The Wandering Press in 2015
Printed in the United States of America

Travels With My Wife is available at a discount
when purchased in bulk for educational or fundraising use,
or by organizations.
For details, email bob@planetbackpacker.net

www.planetbackpacker.net

Cover: Rowing down the Ganges

For Nathan & Chloe

Also by Robert Downes:

Planet Backpacker
Biking Northern Michigan

Our thanks

To Anne Stanton for her expertise in editing this book and for offering many wise suggestions for its improvement. Also to George Foster, good friend and business partner, whose generosity and understanding made all of our travels possible. And to son, Nathan Wildman, for holding down the fort while we were away.

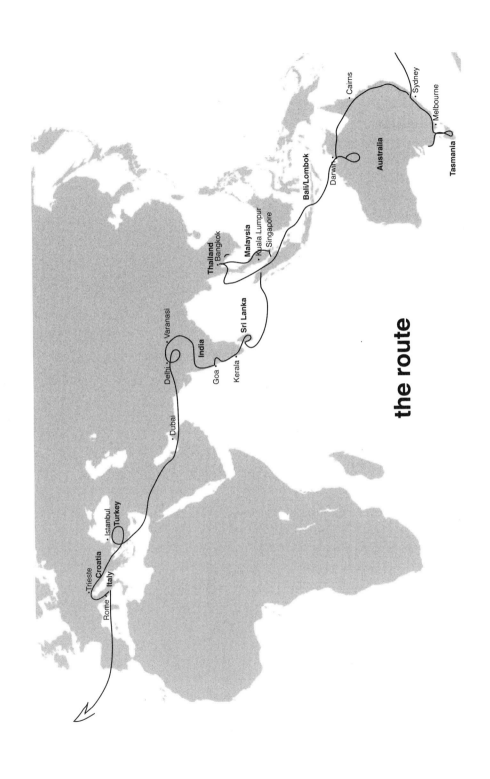

the route

Cairns
Sydney
Melbourne
Tasmania
Australia
Darwin
Bali/Lombok
Thailand
Bangkok
Malaysia
Kuala Lumpur
Singapore
Varanasi
Sri Lanka
Delhi
India
Goa
Kerala
Dubai
Istanbul
Turkey
Trieste
Croatia
Italy
Rome

Contents

Tasmania

Us

"What a lot of traveling you have done in your day, Aunt Augusta."
"I haven't reached nightfall yet," she said. "If I had a companion I would be off tomorrow..."

- Graham Greene • *Travels With My Aunt*

A huge monkey bounds along behind Jeannette as she pedals a rickety bike through the ruins of an ancient city in Sri Lanka. The macacque is as long as a German shepherd from tip to tail, bouncing several feet into the air with every leap, as if flying on truck springs.

Even at a distance, I detect a sense of cunning and purpose on its face as it closes the gap.

"Jeannette, look out!"

Oblivious to the danger, Jeannette rides on, smiling at the swarm of macacques springing on either side of her as we roll past crumbling Buddhas and toppled columns.

I imagine the headlines back home. "American Traveler Mauled by Woman-Eating Monkey," with a sad photo of Jeannette pasted into one of those "gee whiz" squibs you see on the sidebars of the Huffington Post or CNN.com.

Jeannette Wildman, wife, best friend, lover, day care survivor, backpacker, blonde bombshell, and now a potential casualty, turns and spots the critter just as he reaches her rear fender.

But before I can ride to the rescue, the monster bounces away after noting that she has no banana tucked in her skirt. Just another day at the office...

"That sure was a big monkey," she says brightly.

"It had to be the biggest fucking monkey in Sri Lanka," I say. "I thought you were a goner."

The ruins of Anuradhapura glide slowly past the creaking chains of our bikes. Rusty, dusty, neglected bikes not oiled since they left the factory years ago. The noonday sun scissors through our clothing as we roll past a poppy-bright crowd of Buddhist nuns, monks and pilgrims. The February heat of the Equator is the antipode of the ice and snow we've left back home in northern Michigan. A tandoori sun - roasting, relentless, cutting, hammering, eternal.

Strange to think that this long-dead city, which once was home to tens of thousands of people, was dedicated to determining the meaning of existence. As with the dozens of cathedrals, temples and mosques we've encountered around the world, the guardians of Anuradhapura were concerned with where we've been, where we're going, and who or what is to be found in the life beyond the one we're living.

Ahead lies a sacred Bo tree, said to have been propagated from the same tree under which Buddha gained enlightenment 2,500 years ago in India. This cutting was planted by a princess in 288 B.C., and for now, at least, even the monkeys are wise enough to steer clear of its sacred branches.

Dealing with errant monkeys is one of the hazards of traveling through the tropics. Most travelers think that monkeys are cute, and that may be true at a distance of 30 feet or so, but they also have needle-sharp fangs and aren't afraid to use them.

A monkey is inclined to leap on your head if you happen to be sucking on a Coke or have any sort of food on your person. Monkeys also use their feces to repel people they don't care for. While hiking down a beach on another trip, Jeannette had the misfortune to get crapped on by a monkey hanging from a tree; fortunately, the poo washed off as fast as it dribbled on.

Earlier in the day, I made the mistake of shooing one of these thugs with my hat and learned that a monkey doesn't back down in a fight. It bared its two-inch fangs and lunged at me, making me about jump out of my sandals.

And yet, you often see travelers besotted with monkeys, even allowing them to clamber on their shoulders or into the arms of their kids, inviting the possibility of a nasty bite. One jumped up on Jeannette's shoulder back in the Monkey Forest of Bali. I guess they have a sweet tooth for her.

As they say in Asia: no touch monkey.

We're circling Sri Lanka, which is on the rebound from a 26-year civil war that left more than 100,000 dead. Not far north of here, thousands of people are still suffering behind the barbed wire of government concentration camps in the former rebel zone. An island hanging like a mango off the southern coast of India, Sri Lanka is about as far away from the rest of the world as one can get.

For us, the monkey encounter is midway through a seven-month trip around the world that has taken us the length of Tasmania and Australia to Indonesia, Thailand and Malaysia. The months ahead will lead us through India, Turkey, Croatia, Italy and more. And here we are, just the two of us, ready to take on the world and whatever monkeys it may throw at us.

"Someday we'll see the world together" is the dream of a lifetime for many couples and a recurring theme in countless books and films. In the typical film script, a cat burglar husband and wife make their last big score and take it on the lam to see the world together. The final scene has them lounging on a beach in Thailand or Brazil without a care.

If only it were that simple, because of course, most people tend to talk about their dreams, rather than acting on them.

A pity, because traveling around the world is an epic adventure that's possible for the average person to achieve.

You may not have $250,000 or the desire to fly in sub-space on a Virgin Galactic rocket plane. You may not have the cash, know-how or fitness needed to climb Mt. Everest or to sail across the South Pacific. But you can still get a hammock on a barge heading down down the Amazon, bike across Vietnam, or dine on barbequed pig knuckle in Mongolia if you set your heart on getting there.

This is especially true if you go the backpacking route, which cuts travel expenses by as much as 75 percent. This isn't the backcountry camping experience we think of in America. It simply means packing a few necessities into a backpack and bumming around foreign lands on local buses or trains while staying in hostels and cheap guesthouses. Although backpacking as a way of travel has been around since the last Ice Age, it's more relevant than ever in the age of couch surfing and online tools such as Airbnb.com.

It's estimated that there are 100,000 backpackers of all ages traveling the world at any given moment, but it's not hard to imagine that number in Central America alone during January. More likely, there are millions of backpackers out roaming the world, especially in the tropics during the winter months.

With backpacking, you either get it or you don't. If your travel fantasies extend to trailing through the lobby of a Ritz-Carlton behind a cart piled high with new suitcases, forget about backpacking. The reality of the backpacking fantasy often involves clumping through the heat, dust and broken sidewalks of Asian cities or far-off beach towns with two changes of underwear and a few dingy t-shirts in your pack. The goal is to have an intense experience without breaking the bank.

It's possible to travel a great deal and never bump into the backpacking tribe. If you're taking a cruise or staying at an all-inclusive resort, you won't see the dozen or so backpackers passing by on the local bus, heading for a clutch of cheap cabinas on the beach.

But do the math. The typical insanely expensive American vacation of a week at a condo in Hawaii might easily pay for a month of exploring the more interesting environs of Thailand or Latin America, assuming you have the time and inclination.

Taking up the backpacking style of travel was an unexpected transition for me. I had done my share of bumming around in college, hitchhiking across the U.S. and Europe, but by my 30s I suffered from the notion that I was too "grown up" to go romping around the world with a pack on my back, clearly an undignified thing to do once one had reached such an advanced age.

But at the age of 39, I decided to take a solo trip to Spain, Portugal and Morocco, and a backpack seemed a better option than roll-along luggage. Nor did I wish to join a tour full of old folks; I'd travel as the locals did, on buses and trains.

Nonetheless, I felt like a *poseur* standing on the deck of the ferry to Morocco. What the heck was I doing? I was 39 years old, for God's sake! It felt strange walking around the streets of Tangiers, Madrid and Lisbon with a pack on my back like some college kid.

It wasn't until I found myself in a train compartment the size of a bathtub, tangled up with five very skinny, smelly French surfers that I realized I didn't have to grow more fuddy-duddy with age.

The surfers were heading home from Senegal with all of their packs and surfboards jammed into every inch of our compartment, including above our heads. Their bodies and stringy hair flowing past their shoulders were still encrusted with the salt of the sea and the intense body odor it engenders. They were barely out of their teens, three guys and two girls, and they were starving. I bought some food to share and we exchanged a few words in my high school French.

To me, they were living a tantalizing dream, surfing in Africa by day and dancing on the beach at night to the sound of drums. By contrast, my own life seemed pathetic and dull; sitting in a cubicle under fluorescent lights for 40 hours a week, staring at a cathode ray tube and tapping out words I didn't care about.

That was my road to Damascus moment. I embraced my inner vagabond and vowed to start taking the road less traveled.

Jeannette, of course, never had any qualms about traveling around like a college kid with a pack on her back because she's always been a kid at heart. She was just thrilled to travel anywhere when we first met.

She's always been up for an adventure. Years ago, I planned a buddy camping trip to the Grand Canyon with four old friends from high school. It was supposed to be a reunion after not seeing one another for decades. All of my friends agreed to do the hike, yet one by one they dropped out with lame excuses.

There was only one last resort for the "guys only" trip.

"Do you want to hike the Grand Canyon with me?" I asked, somewhat mournfully. At the time Jeannette was running a home day care and it was tough for her to get away.

"Well, sure!" Jeannette said.

"But what about your job?"

"I'll make it happen," she said.

So there went my bright angel and I, hiking down the trail of the same name in the 110-degree heat to the bottom of the canyon. We lay fully-clothed in Bright Angel Creek on the way down in respite from the sun, and on the way back, we rose at 4 a.m. and hiked out beneath a full moon.

And that's how our whole marriage has gone through all of our adventures. I spend months planning our trips and Jeannette is ready to go and up for anything at the drop of a hat.

Embarking on a long-distance trip for months on end is literally a foreign concept in America, where most of us are conditioned to take no more than a week's vacation at a time.

Chances are, if you've got it together enough to plan a lengthy trip and acquire the money to take it, you've also got a work ethic that's hard to shake. Even if you can arrange a sabbatical, you may feel a sense of guilt taking time off from your job, or perhaps a sense of insecurity, considering the unemployment rate of recent years.

So why bother? What could drive you to circumnavigate the earth or wander across its continents for weeks on end? Simply put, to see the glory of our world before you die. To gaze upon its mountains, rivers, oceans, forests, sunsets and cities. To experience the touchstones of history with your own eyes: the pyramids, the Parthenon, the Great Wall. To see the grand parade of its seven billion people milling through the streets from supercities to lowly villages. To explore their markets, enjoy their meals, drink their booze, hear their music, wear their clothes, sleep in their arms, walk in their shoes. To rise with the sun and stroll down the cobblestones of a village in India with an elephant by your side, heading for its morning bath.

Imagine that you are an astronaut landing on a planet of amazing diversity in another galaxy. There, you find blue waterfalls, mushroom trees, flying anteaters and cities of crystal and tin, full of friendly aliens. Would you choose the life of Emily Dickinson and never travel more than a few miles from your landing site, or would you vow to see as much of your new world as possible?

Today, travel also offers you a chance to participate in a global community of wanderers from every corner of the Earth. It's not unusual to find an Indian restaurant in a remote corner of Nicaragua or an Italian crew offering cruises off the coast of Ecuador; a French family running horses in Costa Rica or Ozzies driving down the coast of Chile.

It's also easier than ever to take the trip of your dreams.

Tourism is the number one industry on earth, with more than one billion of us crossing international borders each year. Greasing the wheels of this migration are an endless number of small travel agencies, web sites and adventure travel bureaus poised to handle the logistics of your lodgings, transportation and adrenalin cravings. If you're looking for a beach camp that will let you hang a hammock for $2 per night, there's a website to guide you. If you need to cross half of India, Guatemala or Thailand on an overnight bus, there's a corner travel agency which will have it booked in a snap. And if you crave the company of like-minded souls, there are backpacking tour groups that accommodate singles, couples and travelers of all ages.

Of course, it's one thing to plan a trip around the world and quite another to pull it off if you're a person of ordinary means. In our case, being debt-free was a priority before we hit the road.

Some couples aspire to owning a mini-mansion in the suburbs or a sports car to go with their SUV, but Jeannette and I opted for a modest home that we were able to pay off within 10 years of our marriage.

Consider that the average monthly mortgage payment is more than round-trip airfare for two to anywhere in North America and you can see the value of being debt-free if you've got a traveling bone. For the same reason, I'd chew off my arm before I'd have a car payment. That's good travelin' money, going to waste.

We were also fortunate to have a rare period of calm in our lives to save up; a period of several years where there were no major expenses, college tuition, family disasters, the roof caving in, extensive dental work, major auto repairs, or all of the above. For most of us, that's the prerequisite for living "the dream of a lifetime."

It was 20 years to the week of our first meeting in Traverse City, Michigan that Jeannette and I set out around the world. We met at a square dance, just as my parents had met more than 60 years ago.

Jeannette was sitting by herself in a row of chairs on the far side of an old lumber-era opera house downtown, sniffling over the wreckage of a 12-year marriage that had recently ended. Even 60 feet across the room she seemed to possess a golden aura, as warm as the late afternoon sunlight in Indian summer. The curve of her back was as taut as a hickory bow as I held her in my arms for the first time, whirling her around the old wooden dance floor.

"You've got a strong back," I said for lack of a pick-up line. It was the second thing I ever said to her after "Would you like to dance?" With a torso like an oak, she seemed unusually strong. Still does.

Jeannette's glow would settle over me through all of our years together. And if I happened to see her out walking several blocks away, I'd feel my heart lift with the recognition of her golden hair. And if I bumped into her by accident downtown and caught a glimpse of her sideways, I'd think, what a fine woman that is, even before realizing that she was my wife.

Jeannette has almond eyes with pupils that run kale green at the edges. She's as curvy as any man could desire and prefers dresses and skirts to jeans, but no one would ever call her a "girlie" girl. She is rooted to the earth with the strength of a peasant, yet with the lightness of a honeybee. Her high cheekbones, tawny complexion and a certain glint to her eyes hint at currents of Cherokee blood, rumored to have watered her family tree. She has a thick, blond cascade that must have originated in the genes of East Europe or some Teutonic ancestry. She has a little face compared to my big head, and a snaggle-tooth, wolfie smile that I find adorable.

She's the kind of girl who argues with you over who gets to shovel the roof in the winter and a good dancer to boot. In short, a good catch.

Unfortunately, I committed the classic blunder early on by saying that I thought she'd make "good wife material" as we lingered over dinner.

Jeannette gave me the sort of look you normally see on the face of a doe, ready to run.

"What do you mean?"

Oh-oh.

"I mean, you've got it together with a lot of things. Anyone would be lucky to have you."

"I just got over being married and was sick of it," she said.

"I know, but I'm in a different place than you. I've been single for five years now and I'm starting to think about getting married again."

"I don't know if I want to get married again."

"Well, eventually I'll get married to someone."

I had meant to offer a compliment about what a cool woman she was, but it came out like a bad egg.

But it was true that I thought of her as a prize. Jeannette had worked her way through college with no help from her parents. She had started her own business and was repairing her ramshackle home one room at a time, starting with a leaky roof. Her ex-husband had predicted she'd end up a welfare queen, but she was raising two kids and digging herself out of a tough situation with no help to speak of, not even food stamps, though she was certainly poor enough to qualify. She had no family in the area, nor any grandparents to lend a hand. I thought she had guts - a self-made person who came up from blue collar roots like me with the same kind of dreams - not too big, not too small, but just right.

As for getting married, the thought marinaded between us. Slowly.

We got married five years after our first dance. My proposal was kind of a bust; there was no down-on-a-knee in a restaurant, Jumbo-tron ambush or ring in a wine glass. We looked at engagement rings, deciding that a "blood diamond" was out of the question, and went out to lunch to think about it.

"So, do you want to get married?" I asked as we sat next to each other over chicken pot pies. I don't think I even held her hand.

"I guess so," she said with a little laugh.

"When should we do it?"

"I'm not in any rush. I just got over being married."

Since we were both veterans of past matrimonies gone wrong, there didn't seem to be any rush. So Jeannette wore her rhodolite garnet engagement ring for four years before we said our vows.

"I'm just afraid that marriage will change us," she'd say. "What if it wrecks the good thing we have being single? Plus, I have my kids to think about."

In Jeannette's experience, the map of marriage was like those charts of long ago, which had unknown spaces marked with the legend, "Here be Monsters."

So we took it slow to make sure we knew what we were getting into. It was only many years later that I realized that no one ever really knows what they're getting into when they get married. You just step off a cliff into the dark and find out.

On many nights, we'd sleep in each others arms at Jeannette's place and then I'd tip-toe downstairs while the kids were at breakfast in the back of the house. I'd head out the front door and walk around to knock at the back door for a morning "visit." Nathan and Chloe always looked surprised to see me there so early in the morning, and once, Chloe wondered why I was barefoot.

"I'm trying to be more like Johnny Appleseed," I said.

But eventually, the big day came.

We got married in Jeannette's backyard on a deck she had built for the occasion. Since I'm a deist and Jeannette's an atheist, we arranged for a local shaman to marry us. Nancy specialized in getting her clients in touch with their shamanic power animals. We never did find out what ours were. Chipmunk? Gazelle? But Nancy guaranteed that her weddings lasted forever, and so far, her prophecy has rung true.

Jeannette ticked me off in the lead-up to our wedding. We had seen a gorgeous white lace dress in a store window that seemed perfect for her wedding dress.

"I don't think I like that one," she said after considering it. "I'm too old for a fancy dress like that. Plus, I've got a nice yellow dress in my closet that I can wear and we can save some money."

But she insisted that I rent a tuxedo for the occasion.

"What the hell do I have to rent a tuxedo for if you're going to wear some old yellow dress?" I fumed, imagining some dowdy frock from her hippie college days.

"I want you guys to look good for the wedding," she insisted.

So there I was in a rented monkey suit on a breezy day in May with a snowfall of cherry blossoms showering the deck in Jeannette's back yard. And she walked around the corner, a sight I'll never forget, as beautiful as a fairy princess in that white lace dress.

I vowed that day to try to be a good dad to Nathan and Chloe, and promised that they would remember me more for the laughs and the good times than for being a grouchy stepdad, something I'm still working on with mixed results. I read some flowery vows that Nancy the Wiccan witch had asked us to compose - forgotten as soon as I said them - and when it came time for her turn, Jeannette simply said "Ditto!" and laughed.

We newlyweds settled into the rhythms of our new life together. Long walks or bike rides after work each day. Breakfast in bed every Sunday, reading the *New York Times*. I like cooking as a way to unwind after work, a chore she was happy to surrender. On the other hand, Jeannette loves to play in her garden, while I'm allergic to yard work. What a team! Through the years, Jeannette ran a daycare out of our home, while I was busy editing an alternative newspaper, the *Northern Express Weekly*.

Our rituals took shape. The goodbye kiss, for instance.

Each morning before I leave for work, Jeannette and I share a goodbye kiss and a heart-to-heart hug. They're pecks, really, but each one counts. Our kisses are mandatory, inviolable, because what would happen if I failed to kiss her goodbye and we never saw each other again?

What would happen if failing to kiss her somehow nudged the wheel of fate off track and a bad thing happened? For this reason, I'm also afraid to remove my wedding ring. For all I know, doing so could cause Jeannette to get run over by a truck while crossing the street, or get hit by a falling part from a passing airplane.

On the rare occasions when I'm in a hurry to get somewhere and have to leave, I'll hear Jeannette's muffled voice yelling, "Wait!" from inside the house as her footsteps thump to the door. "Don't you dare leave without your kiss!" she'll say, waving her finger in mock anger.

Other times I'll be a block or two away on my bike and think, oh shit, I forgot my kiss, and turn back, anxious to give and receive. Our kiss isn't just a bond of our love, it's our insurance policy.

Jeannette had a little fun with me in the weeks leading up to our trip around the world. She started hiding a big, black, plastic spider in unexpected places, like in my coffee cup or on my pillow. It was about two inches in diameter and each time I saw it, I'd about jump out of my socks. For variety, she sometimes used a toy snake, hiding it in the salad greens or on top of the coffee pot in the morning.

How can you not love someone like that? We'd have a good laugh and then it was onto the next surprise. She got me every time; it was like experiencing an electric jolt.

What makes a good marriage? I don't know, but it probably has something to do with laughing when someone tricks you over and over again with a toy spider.

Jeannette and I have also managed to have a 20-year conversation that has rarely had a lapse. God knows what we find to talk about - stuff that wouldn't engage the intellect of a monkey, mostly - but somehow we manage to yak on forever. Our talkfest seems to be a key to our 20-year honeymoon.

And on those times when we are on the outs, I remind myself that a good marriage, or a good friendship for that matter, means you have a dozen positive thoughts about the person you love for every negative one that crosses your mind.

Beyond that, for most people on earth, the most important quality in a marriage is having a partner who has their act together.

In the West we've forgotten that marriage is a quasi-business partnership. Love has little to do with the wedlock of billions of young couples in Asia, Africa and other lands where marriages are arranged by parents whose chief concerns are practical matters such as the young man's employment and the other family's means, status and connections.

For much of the world, love is expected to come once the newlyweds get to know each other, if at all. The larger question is whether the bride and groom will produce children and do well enough to support the extended family.

Jeannette and I traveled from the get-go, even when we were broke.. Some people are meant to be nomads, which is perhaps why you're reading this book; you have that wandering gene.

But on our trips of a week or two we began meeting Europeans who were traveling for a month or six weeks at a time. How lucky they were to have such freedom, I thought, while recognizing the trade-offs. For all their freedom, the Europeans typically lived in rented apartments, rather than owning their own homes, which tends to be the case in the U.S.

I can't say when the standard American vacation of one or two weeks began to seem more like tyranny than time off to me, but as we cast a wider net, it began to sink in that there was so much of the world to see and so little time to do it. We were already in our mid-40s by the time we got married. If we tried seeing the world one week at a time each year, we'd be dead before we got through East Europe.

So we decided to embark on a project to see the world piecemeal over a 10-year period in installments of one or two trips per year. I had some help in the matter; as co-owner of a weekly newspaper, I accrued more than 100,000 frequent flyer miles each year by dint of the fact that we paid our massive printing bills off with air-mile credit cards each month.

Our travel project took us first to Costa Rica. Then came Greece, Hong Kong, France, the Virgin Islands, China, Peru, Alaska, Hawaii, Nicaragua, Mexico's Pacific coast, Japan, Guatemala, Belize, South Africa, Mozambique, Costa Rica again, and Brazil.

All of this was done as backpackers. When we traveled 600 miles by bus up the coast of Mexico, or across Belize to Guatemala, or cross-country through Brazil, we were always the only gringos on the bus.

The top-off for our Decade of Travel was supposed to be Jeannette's retirement from 30 years of day care and a two-month camping trip through Australia.

"But we might as well see Sri Lanka while we're on the far side of the world," I said. "And as luck would have it, India is right next door to Sri Lanka."

India? Who knows when we might get back to that far-flung land of mystery and intrigue? It would be criminal not to see it while we were in the neighborhood.

I tossed India on the pile of our travel plans and fell bewitched under the spell of planning our trip. Sooner than you could say "wandering pilgrim" it made perfect sense to travel all the way around the world, taking seven months to get the job done.

That would require months of camping and staying in grungy hostels and ramshackle hotels, mostly through tropical territory in temperatures that were likely to be in the mid-90s or higher. The heat, the bugs, the dirt, crowds, squalor, stink and expense of backpacking around the world... pure heaven to a travel junkie. But it would also mean seven months of being together 24/7, virtually every minute of every day.

I knew that Jeannette loved to travel, and she is enthusiastic to the point of being ferocious.

But at some small level of apprehension it made me wonder if our marriage would survive such a trip. I had read books in which globe-circling lovers had seen their bonds disintegrate from the stress of traveling. *Miles From Nowhere*, for instance, in which author Barbara Savage and her husband bicycled the entire way around the Earth, only to break up when they returned home. I also knew from first-hand experience that traveling through the developing world tends to be more stressful than fun.

Some folks wondered how we'd handle all of those months so tightly bound together in iffy places. You could almost see them shudder at the thought of enduring such a captivity by their own spouses. I could well imagine that a lot of wives wouldn't care for that much togetherness with their husbands, and vice-versa.

Really, how many marriages could survive such a trip? Even I had my doubts.

But Jeannette blew off my misgivings.

"When you're traveling, it's just the two of you against the world," she said. "Plus, all of the things you worry about at home are left behind. I won't have to think about doing the laundry or vacuuming or picking up the grandkids. I can just relax and spend time with the one I love."

What the hell. It was time to have faith and surrender to the dream. And as it turns out, when you're lying in each other's arms with the early morning sun flooding your tent with the song of birds and ocean waves filling your ears on the far side of the world, you feel love at its sweetest sensation. You need her, she needs you; you're adrift in a strange land, counting on each other, and no one else in the whole world knows or cares where you are. Love, I've found, responds to human need; in fact, it comes running, and there are plenty of needs to go around when you're traveling for months on end.

So, to back up a bit, the day finally came when we had saved up, packed up, and wrapped up our act at home to take it on the road. Here's how it all went down.

A Land Down Under

"A lot of people have anxiety attacks when they set out to travel around the world," I say as we wait at the airport. "It's one thing to fantasize about traveling for months on end and another to suddenly find yourself with your support system of family and friends all gone while some drunken beggar is tugging at your sleeve in a bad neighborhood overseas. People say, 'Wait, what have I done?' and freak out."

"Well don't worry about me. I'm not going to freak out, ever," Jeannette says. "After 30 years of day care, this is the 'No More Poopy Diapers Tour' for me. I can't think of a better way to retire and start my new life. It would be a lot harder to just stop working and hang around the house all winter."

"But won't you miss all of your friends and family?" I push.

"No," she says firmly. "When I'm gone, I'm gone, and I can't worry about anyone. When I'm back, I'm back."

This isn't quite true, because in the months ahead, Jeannette will fret a great deal over Nate, Chloe and the grandkids, but for for the time being, it's a good attitude for setting out around the world.

"Well, amen to that, Sugar Shack," I say, employing one of the 100 or so kissy-poo pet names I have for her: Little Bunny, Captain Starfish, Sugarbum Fairy, J'nette, Boojie-Woojie, Sweet Bean...

It's the first of November, time for our getaway from the northern Michigan winter. We'll follow the sun south around the planet, extending our summer by seven months. Not a bad plan.

By 2 a.m. we're leaving Los Angeles for Sydney, Australia, only 7,500 miles to go on a 14-hour flight. Our A380 double-decker airbus is packed with 500-some passengers and crew; it seems a miracle that it will be able to haul this load that distance. Including layovers, from the time we leave home, it will take us a total of 24 hours to reach The Oz as the Down-Under-ers call it.

"It's amazing to think that it took the first Australians seven months to get there," I say. "They were convicts in the late 1700s, chained in leg irons below decks for the whole way in the tropical heat."

But Jeannette is sleeping peacefully beside me as the Pacific slides by, six miles below us in the dark.

Thinking of the convicts isn't much solace, since I'm crammed into the jet's tiny middle seat with a fat lady's blubber spilling over the arm of the chair into my space. My lower back collapsed days before we left and it feels like an ice pick is probing my spine (soon to feel like a sword). I feel like shit.

I start feeling guilty about leaving my job behind for seven months. My best friend, George Foster, and I started the newspaper together more than 20 years ago and now here I am, abandoning ship for the second time in five years for this dubious adventure. I tell myself that no one ever sprawled on their death bed wishing they'd spent more time at the office, but the guilt settles in like a hair shirt that I'll wear for months. For me that's the tough part of leaving: the feeling that I'm letting people down.

The anxiety of leaving home weighs on me like a soggy mattress.

What have I done?

Home Sweet Hostel

Feeling smacked around after the endless flight and the ordeal of passing through customs, we haul our gear past a gauntlet of street people lying propped up on the sticky sidewalk outside the train station in Sydney. Nearby, we find our way to Sydney's Central YHA hostel. It's a multi-story, cavernous affair just shy of Chinatown which offers an industrial-sized kitchen, an adjoining café, and a huge wifi room packed with kids hunched over their laptops.

"Wow, we're old enough to be their parents," Jeannette says, surveying the mob of mostly college-age backpackers in the lobby, waiting to get checked in.

"But that's the good thing about being our age. We're completely invisible to them. See?" I point to a knot of three college girls, barricaded behind a huge pile of packs. "They look right through you, like you're not even there."

"Well, I'm not staying in a dorm."

"Oh, I wouldn't deny you that pleasure. Think of the pillow fights."

"No way. I don't mind staying in a dorm if there's nowhere else to stay, but not here."

I consider the many times I've stayed in hostel dorms, enduring a gamut of snorers, drunks and illegal immigrants. The Nigerian guy in Poland who hadn't bathed in months... the Chinese sailor who looked like he was jumping ship in Anchorage... the little guy from India who kept everyone in the dorm in Budapest awake all night with his snoring. But there have been lots of good times too, rubbing elbows with travelers from Sao Paulo, Northern Ireland, Wichita and Sweden, and the odd experience of waking up with strange women, albeit in different bunk beds with half a dozen other backpackers.

But hostels, it seems, have upscaled their act since those glory days and now offer private rooms. Jeannette's fears of bunking with a clutch of chatty 20-year-olds are allayed with the flutter of my soon-to-be-limpid credit card. Privately, I imagine that sooner or later we'll be biting that dorm bullet for lack of other options.

Unless you're as rich as Jay Z or are staying in a tent, hostels offer the only realistic lodgings for long-range travelers on a budget.

Although some cater exclusively to youth (particularly in beach towns), most hostels today welcome guests of all ages, from teens to those in their 70s. Lodgings are paid for on a sliding scale, with a bunk in a dorm of 10 beds being the cheapest, on up to private rooms that cost three times as much, per person.

Even if you have enough money to stay exclusively at B&Bs or small hotels, there are good reasons for long-haul travelers to opt for hostels. There's the social aspect of people-watching, sharing experiences and trading information with other travelers. Hostels also have bulletin boards, local excursions, book exchanges, communal kitchens and sometimes, lively bars.

For the first-timer, the website hostelworld.com makes it possible to book rooms in advance and survey a range of options down the road, including B&Bs, beach camps and budget hotels.

Land of the $19 Hamburger

Being the leader of our two-person expedition means sharing my great wisdom about the backpacking lifestyle.

"Now that we're backpacking around the world our 'job' is to walk for about 10 hours a day to see the sights because we'll go crazy if we don't have something to do with our time," I tell Jeannette. "We need to have some kind of work to do to keep our sanity, and walking tends to be it."

"Works for me, I love to walk," she says. "Let's get up in the morning and walk 'til the sun goes down every day."

No kidding. Jeannette can walk me down to a nub. As mentioned earlier, she's of the earth. Soon, I'm eating my words regarding that bit about walking 10 hours a day.

"I just want to walk up around that point and back," Jeannette says by late afternoon, pointing to a distant bend along the bay as I'm blue-lipped and ready to drop from exhaustion. She shows no sign of slowing down as we walk from one tree laden with violet blooms to another.

I throw a tantrum. "Give me a fucking break, I'm beat. Exhausted. You go," I wave. "I'm sitting here on this bench."

Anyone else would have said, "Oh, quit your damn whining and come on." But with characteristic cheer and good grace (and a stubbornness worthy of a mule) Jeannette gives me her innocent look and says, "Sweetie, you just wait here and rest, I'll be right back."

Soon enough, I'm trailing in Jeannette's wake another mile out and back, marveling at her machine-like stamina. Grudgingly.

And then? More walking, on into the night.

It's in Sydney that I have doubts about my ability as the "expedition leader."

"I can't seem to find my way around the block!" I say in exasperation as we wander around in a fruitless search for our hostel.

"Don't you remember passing that sign back there?" Jeannette says. "Our place is back that way past the railroad tracks."

"Everything looks the same to me, and I can't even seem to read the map," I say. "I'm not even sure which end of town we're in."

"It's right around that corner and down that road," Jeannette points.

"Cripes, I'm used to thinking that *you* don't know where you're going, and now I'm the ding-a-ling without a direction. How are we going to find our way around the entire world if I can't even get around Sydney?"

"I'll be your compass from now on," she says with a smile.

Sure enough, Jeannette manages to guide us around Sydney for the next few days while my sense of direction has gone on vacation.

"Do you think I've got Alzheimers disease?" I wonder.

"Oh sure, that must be it. I can tell by all the silly stuff you're saying."

The famed Sydney Opera House is a bit underwhelming. Its cascade of clamshells looks as big as a football stadium in photos, but that turns out to be an optical illusion.

"It sure is a lot smaller than I thought it would be," Jeannette says as we stroll around the outside of the building. "It seems almost dinky."

Sacrilege, but true. Eight months ago I got the bright idea to buy tickets to the opera, reasoning that we weren't likely to be popping back into Sydney in the years to come. I shelled out $350 to surprise Jeannette with tickets to "Don Giovanni" by Mozart. A monstrous expense.

Unfortunately, the opera is on the evening of our arrival in Sydney after 24 hours in transit. After walking all over town and downing a couple of beers, we're staggering like zombies by the time the show starts.

The plot is a downer: Don Juan seems to be an obsessive-compulsive rapist who "seduces" women at any cost. Mozart's script has much the same finesse as a porn film, and a bad one at that. People in the audience laugh because they know they're expected to.

"You'd get 20-to-life in prison if you acted like Don Juan back home," I whisper.

"I can't keep my eyes open," Jeannette yawns. "They're like garage doors slamming shut."

"Me too. Feels like I'm dying."

"Just don't start snoring," she says as we pinch each other to stay awake through the Don's shenanigans.

We get mugged right off by the Exchange Rate Bandit. The $1,000 U.S. in my wallet buys just $890 Australian.

"Our money sucks! Same story all over the world."

This is not happy news, because it turns out that things are crazy expen sive in the Oz, and we quickly learn that Sydney is one of the most expensive cities in the world.

A sit-down dinner in a restaurant is almost inconceivable on our backpacking budget. After marching around to a dozen harbor-side cafés we conclude that a burger and fries cost $19 on average, and a small Thai chicken salad goes for $30, three times what we'd expect to pay back home. We settle on a seafood take-out stand and dine on a bench with a view of the Harbor Bridge. It's the start of our long acquaintance with street vendors and meals from grocery stores.

I start writing down every single expenditure throughout the day in a notebook, a practice that we'll follow for the entire trip.

"It's kind of scary how much we're spending from the get-go," I say, thinking of our hostel room that runs $70 per night for a couple of narrow bunk beds.

"Aren't things a lot cheaper in Asia?" Jeannette asks. "We just have to make it until then."

"Yeah, but I'm wondering if we'll get that far if all of Australia is as expensive as Sydney."

"Well, we can always go home."

"I don't think that's an option."

Into the Blue Mountains

A side trip to the Blue Mountains outside Sydney puts my transportation plans to a test. It turns out they are crap, especially since we are packing enough junk to outfit a 19th century safari.

We arrived in Australia with a large rolling duffel bag, about four feet long and two-and-a-half feet wide, stuffed with camping gear. This includes our tropical sleeping bags, ThermaRest sleeping pads, a 4-person tent (extra space for comfort), folding chair pads, JetBoil stove, cooking gear, plates, cups, cutlery and dozens of small items such as mini-lanterns, chargers, cords, duct tape, clothes pins, felt towels, all-purpose liquid soap, cameras and our iPad. To top it off, we've got a smaller tent for a six-day hike through the mountains of Tasmania, along with a separate backpacking stove and rain gear expressly for that trip.

It has taken six months of careful shopping, comparing and whittling down to put together our gear, and now here it is, packed in a rolling duffel bag with my indispensable backpacking guitar lashed on top to boot.

This is on top of the two large backpacks Jeannette and I have strapped to our backs, also stuffed with clothing, hats, sunscreen, bug-bite remedies, first aid kits, ponchos and more.

For security and backup, I've got $1,000 cash in a cheap-looking money belt, with the $100 and $50 denominations all dated 2004 or later to ward off concerns about counterfeiters (bills with dates after 2004 contain elements that aren't easily copied).

I've also uploaded copies of our passports along with our credit card numbers and their emergency contacts to my email in case everything we own gets ripped off. The card numbers are scrambled in case my email gets hacked.

Additionally, I keep my wallet in my front pocket, attached by a chain to my belt.

In short, the usual precautions.

Having had my pocket picked once before on a subway in Lisbon, I know it's foolish to assume that one is too street-smart to get plucked while traveling. The bad guys do this for a living, after all, and usually have nothing to lose.

Waiting for a bus at Brazil's Iguazu Falls a year ago, Jeannette and I were talking to a college student who'd been traveling around the country for weeks. We assumed he was a savvy traveler by dint of the long list of destinations he checked off, but Jeannette noticed that the lining of his back pocket was hanging out.

Sure enough, his wallet had been stolen from his rear pocket, possibly just minutes before while we were waiting in line.

"Why in the world would anyone who travels keep their wallet in their rear pocket?" Jeannette wondered as he ran off looking for the thief.

Many long-range travelers in Australia buy a used car for a few months, selling it when their trip is done. Often, this means taking a huge loss.

Our plan, mad as it turns out, is to take buses around the country in order to meet the natives and have a more sociable time. This would save us a huge amount of money over the option of buying a car.

I studied the car purchase option at length in the year prior to our trip and learned that, a) these cars tend to be 15-year-old junkers with at least 150,000 miles on the odometer for ridiculous asking prices; and b) there are government hassles in the way of fees, inspections and licensing to deal with, not to mention, c) the likelihood that your junk car will break down for a costly repair before you sell it, if you can, and d) the high cost of gasoline in Australia.

So, back in Michigan, browsing the options on the Internet, it looked like taking the bus was the best way to see Australia, and in fact, many people do, with a wide range of backpacker bus options available.

The problem is, these bus-bound vagabonds tend to be college-age kids hopping from hostel-to-hostel on a well-trammeled circuit, where the lodgings tend to be dormitories and the impulse is to party-til-you-puke each night. We're decades past that age and inclination.

In Sydney, I share my bus idea with the owner of a rental car place and, as might be expected, he pooh-poohs it.

"I've been to America and you couldn't camp there very easily while traveling on a bus, now could you?" he says. "It's no different in Australia."

But I'm not willing to throw in the towel yet, so we roll our gypsy baggage onto a bus, then a train, and make the 60-mile trip out of town to Katoomba and the Blue Mountains.

It's here that my plan starts to fall apart. It's about a two-mile hike from the train station to the campground outside town, and it's soaking hot under the 90-degree sun.

Along the way we catch sight of a giant black spider, munching on a dead bird.

"Do you think that was some kind of rubber spider they put out for Halloween?" Jeannette asks a block later.

"Hon, I don't think they have Halloween in Australia."

"That couldn't have been real."

"Yeah, but it was. Try not to think about it."

Sweating as if in a steam bath, we haul our rolling duffel bag and backpacks into the campground down a long hill on the far side of town, the only ones there without a car.

"I think maybe we should ditch the bus plan," Jeannette says cautiously.

"I think you may be right."

That night we also find that the soil of Australia tends to be as hard as concrete, owing to the dryness of the continent. We bend every stake we own when a high wind blows down our tent. Well after midnight, I scramble outside and use a new knife to anchor some lines against the wind, but even with its razor-sharp blade it barely pierces the earth.

The Blue Mountains are so named because they're colored a misty blue by the haze of billions of microscopic oil drops evaporating from the eucalyptus trees on their slopes. It's the same sort of haze that gives the Smoky Mountains their allure in Tennessee, only with a torrid, tropical twist.

We spend a couple of days hiking deep into canyons filled with 200-foot gum trees and 20-foot tall umbrella ferns which have lingered on since the days of the dinosaurs. You wouldn't be surprised to see a diplodoccus or stegasaurus walk around the corner at any moment. Instead, there are flocks of white cockatoos, parrots, and the dirt-scratching Lyre bird that has a tail which sweeps up like Liberace's hairdo. The constant plowing of these birds in search of bugs helps propagate the forest.

Our greatest discovery, however, is the barbie we find at our campground, Australia's gift to hungry travelers.

Barbies are gas or electric-powered grills found in virtually every campground and public park in the country. They make it possible to shop at supermarkets instead of restaurants, saving hundreds of dollars as you "toss another shrimp on the barbie."

We also make our first acquaintance with Australia's celebrated flies. Our barbeque of steak sandwiches is a rallying cry for hundreds of flies which descend on a dinner we've been slavering over in anticipation. Instead, nature unleashes bug hell. We spend the entire meal waving with one hand and wolfing down our food with the other.

"Truly a meal to remember," Jeannette says.

Stringybark Creek

We haven't given up on the bus quite yet; we catch a coach to the town of Bright, a cycling mecca about 400 miles south of Sydney. Jeannette gazes out the window much of the way, hoping to catch sight of a kangaroo, but no such luck.

"I thought Australia was supposed to be swarming with kangaroos," she says sadly.

"Well, it's like the deer back home When you try to see one, they're nowhere around; but when you least expect it, they pop out at you."

But Australia's wildlife slowly reveals itself. The next day, a snake rimmed with bands of copper and olive flashes under Jeannette's tire like a whipcrack as we ride along a bike path south of Bright. It's nearly four feet long.

"Oh, that's a small one," a cyclist named Glen tells me as we roll along on rental bikes past vineyards and gum trees in a peloton of riders.

"I've heard that Australia has the most poisonous snakes and spiders in the world," I reply. Back home, I had read up on Australia's menagerie of two-steppers, vipers and big brown spiders that leave ulcerating, flesh-eating wounds leading to a painful death.

"Oh, you learn to avoid them," Glen says with a dismissive air. "As for spidahs, I'm an electrician by trade and have wiggled through all sorts of crawl spaces. I've never had a problem with a spidah."

Turns out that most of Australia's venomous snakes dwell in the desert void of the Outback, and few people die in an age when antivenins are common. There's a widespread claim that a teenage girl was bitten on the buttocks some 15 years ago while squatting to take a pee and was too embarrassed to report it until it was too late. But this is possibly an urban legend, since the official stats show that only four Ozzies were killed by snakes in the 2000s, none of them being a teenage girl.

Reportedly, 80 percent of snake bites in Australia are caused by someone trying to kill a snake, which gets understandably tetchy.

A snake bite is treated by wrapping the wound tightly in an elastic bandage and then supporting it in a sling until the victim can be taken to a hospital for a shot of antivenin. One should never suck the poison from the wound as advised in old Western movies, because this will deliver a shot of venom straight to the brain, possibly killing the would-be rescuer in minutes.

But I'm glad we didn't have to test this form of emergency care on Jeannette, since the snake's head was only inches from her leg.

Jeannette and I are bicycle junkies, so Bright is on our list of "must do" destinations.

Nestled in the shadow of Australia's version of the Alps, Bright is a premier camping destination and the trailhead of a 40-mile bike path, said to be the best in the country. We spend two days cycling through the wine country, drinking our share of the local Shiraz.

Spring is a dream in Australia. We ride our bikes through an avenue of Sapphire Dragon trees and breathe in the fragrance of creamy violet flowers, hanging in tens of thousands of blooms from their limbs. We spot four kookaburras up in an old gum tree, laughing at us as we ride by. How gay their life must be.

Bright is packed with German tourists. Sometimes it seems like there are more Bavarians in the Oz than Australians. We've run into scads of German, Austrian and Dutch travelers so far, but no Americans.

Nonetheless, the Australians are able to tell our nationality within seconds of hearing our bland accents. As Americans, we elicit no comments, which strikes me as strange, since in our country, a passing Australian would be peppered with a dozen questions. Maybe we Yanks are more common than I imagine.

Not far from here is the poetic-sounding Stringybark Creek. It was here in 1878 that Austrialian/Irish bushranger Ned Kelly gunned down three policemen disguised as prospectors who were on his trail.

Kelly roamed this country in the 1870s, robbing banks with his gang. Gold had been discovered in this alpine valley in 1850, and thousands of Chinese laborers were brought in to dredge the Oven River aboard vast engines that crawled through the current, scooping, digesting and excreting the riverbed. The coolies and the Aborigines who once lived here are now long gone, as is the gold.

Kelly was either a vicious thug or a Robin Hood-style outlaw hero, depending on which reading of history you choose to believe, traditional or revisionist. But after killing the posse sent to fetch him, he and his gang were cornered by an army of cops in 1880. He chose to shoot it out with an iron bucket on his head and a steel plate armoring his chest. They shot the legs out from under him, took him to Melbourne for a kangaroo court trial and a hanging, and used his skull for a paperweight. Now, of course, he is much celebrated, like Billy the Kid in America.

Heading south for Melbourne on the night train from Wangaratta, I gush about Australia being the finest country in the world.

"The infrastructure of trains, buses and ferries are top notch and the cities are so safe and clean. And the Australians are so fit and friendly," we agree, blah, blah, blah...

But we arrive in Melbourne at 9:30 p.m. and for a moment, I think I might have to drop my pack and pop some young drunk on his ass who starts hassling us as we make our way through the train station.

"My girlfriend dumped me," he sobs as we ride up an escalator. "That's whoy I got me drinks."

We find our hostel down a dark alley in the rain, closed for the night. Fortunately, someone lets us in and we rouse the caretaker; otherwise, we would have been out in the rain at 11 p.m. without any options but to sleep in a doorway. Once again, Fortune loves a fool who travels.

Our next hotel in Melbourne is a step down. "It's the seediest place in town," a passerby advises us when we ask for directions. The rug in the hallway smells of vomit and urine and the walls of our room are dingy with the grime of having gone unpainted for decades.

"But as dumps go, it's not that bad," Jeannette says charitably.

"It's not as bad as the Tokyo Hotel," I admit; the old haunt of traveling blues musicians in downtown Chicago is our standard for measuring the depths of abysmal lodgings.

It turns out that Melbourne's nightlife comes alive at around 11:30 p.m., and the streets are packed with kids heading for the nightclubs. We're serenaded by a succession of off-key street singers, braying until 5 a.m. beneath our window.

"Where the heck are the earplugs?" I groan as the clock ticks past 3 a.m.

Morning Ritual

Our first rental car in Australia has me driving on the "wrong" side of the road for the first time in my life in one of the most bass-ackward cities in the world. Melbourne is infamous for its confusing traffic rules, even among Ozzies. I sideswipe a tree on the way out of town and run up on a curb, but we manage to make it to a campsite far down the coast on the Great Ocean Road.

The Great Ocean Road threads its way along the coast of southern Australia, midway up a wall of high cliffs. It's considered one of the most spectacular drives in the world. It was constructed with pick-axes, wheelbarrows and dynamite by veterans of World War I in an attempt to rival the drive along the French Riviera or Highway 1 in California.

This road was also meant to serve both as a memorial to WWI vets from Down Under and to provide them with jobs. The brutal work of chipping a route along the cliffs was intended to rehabilitate damaged men back into society after the horrors of the war.

Consider, for instance, the legless soldier in the song, "And the Band Played Waltzing Matilda." He was so mutilated in the Turkish battle of Gallipoli that he "thanked Christ there was nobody waiting for me, to grieve, to mourn, and to pity," when his troop ship pulled back into Sydney Harbor. These were the men who built this road.

Far down the road, colossal waves break against the knees of the 12 Apostles, a thicket of stone pillars that tower hundreds of feet above the sea. Across the Bass Strait lies Tasmania, the last stop in the great Southern Ocean before Antarctica.

We awaken to the cackle, shrieks and warble of tropical birds each morning - parrots, magpies, kookaburras and cockatoos with crowns like a spray of celery leaves. Their chatter reminds us of monkeys as the morning sun fills our tent.

Camping has its joys and breakfast alone makes a good case for tenting your way across Australia. We drink hand-pressed filter coffee each morning along with some variation on mango or passionfruit yogurt. Our toast is blackened over the butane flame of a backpacking stove. For company, a white, sulphur-crested cockatoo lands on our picnic table, tugging at a loaf of bread.

Lorne is a pricey beachside resort and the home of Steve, a fellow backpacker I met a few years ago in Egypt when he was halfway through a nine-month trip around the world. Steve is the head chef at the town's finest restaurant, parked on a gorgeous beach adorned with surfers and coastal pines.

"So, how do you like Australia?" he asks over lunch.

"We love it, it's so beautiful here, but it's very expensive compared to what we're used to," Jeannette says.

We tell Steve our sad tales of $19 sandwiches and the beer that cost us $18 in Bright, three times what you'd pay in the U.S.

"Things are expensive because wages and the cost of food are high," Steve says. "In the summer, I can't get kitchen help or waiters unless I pay $20 or $25 an hour."

"Our daughter only gets $2.50 an hour, plus tips," Jeannette says, thinking of Chloe working back home at a diner.

"Yes, but tipping is almost unknown in Australia," Steve says. "The restaurant has to make up for it by charging more. Add in overhead and taxes and at best, the restaurant makes 10 percent on every meal, even though entrees run $45 in the main section."

Steve tells us that some Australians pay up to $7,000 per week to rent summer getaways in Lorne, more than most people on Earth earn in a year.

Later, I spot some graffiti in a beachside bathroom: "Make the politicians work for $15 an hour and see how they like it," it states defiantly. I reflect that this is more than double the minimum wage in the U.S., yet here in the pricey Down Under, the minimum wage of $15 per hour is considered intolerable and insulting.

Steve works up to 16 hours per day, six days a week. He keeps a hawk eye on the operation of the restaurant as we talk and seems overworked and stressed. The massive workload has eroded the happy-go-lucky backpacker I partied with on the Nile. But he has a trip in the works to drive around the American West for several weeks, which I imagine will prove restorative. Sometimes you have to get lost to find yourself again.

We edge closer to the wild side of Australia. Lost on a dirt road, we careen to a stop as a koala lumbers across our path and scrambles up a gum tree, falling on his ass as the bark shreds away. He scrambles back up the tree and gazes down on us with his teddy bear eyes, as awestruck of us as we are of him.

The koala is a quizzical beast which has nothing in common with a true bear. As with many Australian mammals, it's a marsupial, meaning their young are born in an embryonic state and incubated in a pouch. The koala joey rides around in mamma's pouch for as long as seven months.

Although it looks cute and cuddly, a koala has a set of long sharp teeth and claws, ideal for climbing the eucalyptus trees where it spends its lifetime, munching on leaves. Koalas are also great bellowers during the mating season from September to March, emitting lusty snoring sounds, which alert females in the area to their relative size, with the idea being that "bigger is better." Male koalas sometimes resort to rape when they encounter females who are unwilling or not yet in heat.

Rough sex seems to be the norm for these teddy bears; a lot of bellowing and screaming takes place when koalas mate, and the male may have to excuse himself from his amours to fight off other suitors.

That night we hike down a long hill by a river at dusk to gaze at a mob of 30 to 40 kangaroos, bouncing through the tall grass in the half-darkness, light as feathers floating on the spring of their legs.

"Can you imagine what it was like to have been an Aborigine?" Jeannette says as we watch the kangaroos watching us beneath the rising moon. "This is like a scene out of 20,000 years ago."

"I'm sure they had many pleasant meals of kangaroo tail," I say. But I too am awestruck by the beauty of this primal scene as the hoppers melt into the darkness far across the field.

We wrap up the Great Ocean Road in Port Fairy, a town renowned for its two dozen shipwrecks and an old fort that guarded Australia from an invasion by the Russians in the 1800s. The hulks of old naval cannon emplacements remain pointed toward the sea, waiting for the invasion that never came. Two hundred years ago, with the rest of the undeveloped world already divided up by the British, Germans, French and Belgians, the Russians had considered invading Australia for their own piece of colonial pie.

The irony here is that the Ozzie cannons are pointed south towards Antarctica, whereas the Russians would have had to sail from the far north of Siberia, all the way around the great Down Under to get here. It seems a bit of a stretch.

"I'd love to get a Port Fairy t-shirt," Jeannette says. The town's name is tailor-made for such a trophy, which is what backpackers collect as "part of the job" of traveling around the world. Alas, we walk all over town without spotting one. The souvenir t-shirt seems to be a rare species in the Oz.

Tasmania

Every American of a certain age knows about Tasmania, but only because one of the characters in the old Bugs Bunny cartoon series was a Tasmanian devil who came and went as a frenzied whirlwind. Younger Americans, perhaps, know nothing at all; it wouldn't surprise me if only one in 20 of my countrymen could place Tassie on a map. Perhaps not even one in 50.

"It's kind of an expensive side trip, but it's one of those places at the end of the Earth that you just have to visit," I say.

"You're my tour guide," Jeannette says. "I just let you make the plans."

"Well, since we're in the neighborhood..."

Tasmania hangs off the teats of Australia on the far end of the world. We had hoped to take a ferry to the island, but, inexplicably, the cost of a slow boat across the Bass Strait is twice that of a trip by plane. We had also planned to rent bikes and ride down the east coast of Tasmania, but stumbling around various websites led us to the tantalizing prospect of hiking the Overland Track.

The Overland Track is a 45-mile trail through the wilderness at the northern center of the island, considered one of the top 10 hikes in the world. During the summer, hordes of hikers arrive here every day from around the world, although their numbers are divvied out by the park rangers. No more than 60 hikers are allowed to begin the trail each day.

The trail is not without its perils. Heatstroke is a possibility during the summer months, which start in November at this end of the globe, and snowstorms are likely the rest of the year. If you're 20 miles into the trail, there's no ranger waiting around to rescue you and no phone service either. The park authorities warn that you can get yourself in a life-and-death situation pretty quick out in the bush. It turns out they're not kidding.

"Help!"

Blasts of an icy wind blow Jeannette off her feet three times under the weight of her heavy pack on the climb up Cradle Mountain within an hour of starting our hike. We slip along the slope of the mountain with our ponchos flapping like wings, pummeled by a sideways rain whipping at what feels like 60 mph. The valley far below is smothered in fog.

"I can't believe how strong the wind is!" Jeannette says, soaked but smiling.

We scramble up a network of chains, pulling ourselves 1,500 feet up the mountain in a light drizzle that turns into a downpour. A couple of miles on we find an old wooden hut and don our rain suits, but by then we're soaked to the bone, our hands are numb with cold, and there's snow on the ground. The wind, rain and fog conceal what must be a magnificent view as we stumble along through a stream and a jungle of rocks that makes up the trail.

These mountains can be cruel. In 1824, eight convicts from a remote British labor camp at Macquarie Harbour escaped into the southern half of this range. Fifteen days into the escape, the starving men drew lots to determine who would be killed for food with their lone axe. Three terrified men turned back, but the rest wandered for weeks, lost among these grim peaks. One by one, the survivors killed the weakest and the lame among them, devouring their flesh.

In the end, there were only two, each afraid to fall asleep, fearing that the other would seize the axe. Irish convict Alexander Pearce stayed awake the longest and made the cut, so to speak.

Pearce was a little guy, standing just 5-foot-2, but was said to be a tough, wiry cannibal. At one point, he had been on the escapees' list as next in line for dinner, but fortunately (for him), another convict suffered a snake bite on his foot and was substituted as the main course after it became clear he wouldn't recover.

After reaching the frontiers of civilization, Pearce joined a band of bushrangers engaged in a sheep-stealing ring. Upon his capture, he confessed to cannibalism, but the authorities thought it was a preposterous tale and didn't believe him. A year later he escaped again with another young convict, who was quickly dispatched for dinner. Pearce was captured with some of his mate's body parts in his pockets, and this time he swung for it.

At his 1824 hanging in Hobart, Pearce left us with this culinary advice: "Man's flesh is delicious. It tastes far better than fish or pork." He was dissected upon his death, and today his skull is a museum piece held by the University of Pennsylvania.

After four to five hours of hiking through the rain, the Waterfall Hut hoves into view and we bed down with more than 20 other hikers on plywood bunks. Jeannette and I are grateful that we purchased sets of longjohns at a camp store in Launceton prior to making the hike, because we're chilled to the bone in our wet clothes.

There are eight stove-heated huts in the park for those lucky enough to arrive in time; otherwise, you're stuck tenting it out on a damp platform. Fortunately, we began our hike two weeks before the semi-official start of the hiking season and there's still space for us to stretch out our sleeping bags.

The high fee required to hike the trail seems like chicken feed once we take the comfort of the huts into account; they sure beat camping in the rain. The huts offer a common kitchen along with dormitories of plywood bunks crammed with hikers. Each hut is equipped with a small furnace piled high with dozens of soaking, muddy boots and funky socks. It makes for a fungy, unappetizing odor, but who can complain when the state of one's socks are at stake?

That night, a friendly wombat comes calling, sniffling around the camp. The wombat is a groundhog about the size of a young pig with a quizzical expression on its face and an armored butt that protects it from harm when it burrows into its den. Like the koala and the wallaby, it is indescribably "cute."

"The wombat is one of Australia's greatest mysteries," a fellow hiker tells us. "No ones knows how it produces perfectly square pieces of dung out of its round arsehole."

The trail turns into a stream the next day as the rain floods down from the mountains. We walk for hours through ankle-deep water and mud, often through fields of thousands of rocks, boulders and rotting timber ties, which offer 10,000 opportunities for a hard fall with a heavy pack. I am chagrined to think that I didn't obtain traveler's insurance for this end of the trip because of my belief in Australia being a safe country. Hopefully, we won't need to be medevac'd out of here due to a broken limb.

On and on we climb through the undulating hills, wading through cold mud, our boots completely soaked and caked with an inch of black frosting.

Taking a break, I notice something wriggling on my gear, Satan's black spermatozoa by the look of it; a two-inch leech, writhing like an inchworm, blindly stabbing out for blood. At a stop up ahead, a hiker from France reveals a leg streaming red from where he's been nailed by one of these suckers. He foolishly ripped the leech from his flesh instead of letting it take its fill. You can't pull them off because that produces a bleeding wound from the anti-coagulate gunk they secrete, whereas a sated leech drops off your body. It reminds me to fetch a vial of sea salt from my pack, which I prepared for just such situations.

Jeannette and I both suffer leech bites further on up the trail and I apply my sea salt remedy, mixed with a little water. Within 30 seconds the leeches shrivel up and drop off. Nice. The salt option works like a charm.

Thirteen miles into the next day's hike, the trail ends in a deep pond of mud before climbing higher. Splash, splash, splunk. At times the ankle-deep mud is impossible to walk around. We're weaving with exhaustion by the time we reach the Pelion Hut on the edge of a plain teeming with wildlife.

There, we spot a wallaby straight off with a joey in its pouch. He's about a third the size of his mama, but has no trouble crawling into her pouch as she nibbles the grass. Baby joey may live in his mama's pouch for as long as nine months before he feels safe enough to venture outside.

Half of the hikers at Pelion are hearty Tasmanian and Australian men of middle age who are doing an annual buddy hike together.

"Oh, this is nothing," says one of their party when Jeannette remarks on the mud. He's tall as a tree and a member of the Australian Air Force on leave with his mates for their annual trek. "We've been up to the Top End (of Australia) where you can hardly fight your way through the rainforest, and also to Papua, New Guinea, which was a real bugger. You're crawling through the mud and the snakes and the giant spidahs there. I had my doubts we'd get back from that one."

His group is well-prepared with heavy rain pants and gaiters to keep their boots dry, something I dearly wish we had acquired, since they are able to simply splash through the mud without picking their way around it. The rest of us are couples from many lands: Sweden, Germany, France, Switzerland, Venezuela, China and mainland Australia.

A couple of Swedes as big as sasquatches stumble into the lodge, strapped with a truckload of gear for a trip around the world. They're both in their mid-to-late 60s and have had a rough time of it.

"My wife, she fell," her husband says, pointing at his stricken companion.

His wife had endured a full-eagle face-plant in a mud bog, laden with a chest pack in addition to the dangling gear strapped to her mammoth backpack. She was soaked head-to-toe in the stinking, black ooze.

"Oh! I am not happy mit dis," she mutters, and we believe it. Jeannette shows her the way to a bathing spot in a nearby stream.

It's near this hut that several hikers spot a large tiger snake coiled up by the trail. It's estimated to be six-feet long. The Overland Track is literally crawling with these poisonous snakes, but they're a timid bunch and no one has died of snake bite here since 1950.

Still, they do make one a bit nervous and I tap with my walking stick as we wander through the bush. We hear the occasional slither, but happily, the snakes remain shy.

Day four. Nothing says Thanksgiving quite like dehydrated beef teriyaki for two, scooped out of a boiler bag with our plastic sporks. The beef has the taste and consistency of cardboard, or perhaps pencil erasers, in a sauce of sweet, gooey rice. Fresh, untreated rainwater with a birdshit bouquet collected from the roof of our hut makes for an adequate beverage, although we would prefer a nice Tasmanian Chardonnay. Dessert is from our precious horde of dates.

"Think of all our friends back home eating their turkey and cranberries while we're sitting here under the sky, surrounded by mountains," Jeannette says as we squat on a tent platform.

"Well, at least we get to dine al fresco."

We started our day slaving like coolies under heavy loads up the side of a mountain. My pack can't weigh over 40 pounds but it feels like 100. Jeannette is packing maybe 25 pounds., trucking along like a mule without a care. By trail's end, we bathe in an icy stream at a waterfall, washing away the patina of mud and sweat.

"I stink like a boy!" Jeannette says.

"Well, I'm grateful you don't look like one."

The Lost World

Tasmania has an unworldly feel to it for good reason. Located at the southern end of the world, its evolutionary path developed along different lines than the rest of the planet. Here are bulbous trees, pineapple-shaped bushes and odd animals, such as the echidna, a palm-sized spiny anteater that folds into itself like a turtle when threatened.

The Overland Track was blazed by a hunter of wombats and possums named Bert Nichols who roamed this wilderness for decades, starting in the 1920s. Part Aborigine, he carved out the Overland Track for tourists in the 1930s, although it was years before anyone would dare hike it without taking him along as a guide. Even today you can get lost if you stray off the trail; one woman walked across the plain at Pelion Hut a few years back, climbed a mountain and was never seen again.

Our final day finds us hiking nine miles in the rain. This last stretch is a brushy jungle said to be heavily infested with tiger snakes and I bump the earth with a twisted stick the entire way, hoping the vibration will scare them off.

At last we come a'shivering to a rough old wooden hut, which measures about 14 by 14 feet. With its soggy planks and mossy roof, it looks like the home of a fairy tale witch.

"Wow, who knew that a coal stove could be so hard to light?" I say to Jeannette. We're the first ones to reach this gloomy place and the rusty stove looks to be 100 years old. I spend 45 minutes soaking the chunks of shining black rock with coal oil again and again, trying to ignite them without effect. This includes roasting the coal with the burner of my backpacking stove turned up full blast.

"I think we've got about three matches left," Jeannette says. "And soggy ones at that."

But by the grace of God the coal finally lights to relieve the misery of our being chilled to our soaking bones.

Soon, there are 10 of us crammed into a hut designed for eight, which is said to be the lair of possums and rats at night. Our wet clothing and packs hang from the rafters like hams in a smokehouse while the rest of our packs, cooking gear and muddy boots cram every inch of the muddy floor. Some of the hikers elect to sleep three to a bunk, so no one has to sleep on the filthy plank floor with the varmints. One lucky guy is accepted as a sandwich by two young women. We fall asleep by 9 p.m., straining to hear the scramble of possums and rats.

The next morning I catch hell from one of our fellow backpackers for rinsing our coffee grounds into the mud outside the hut.

"But it's organic," I protest. "It's compost."

"It doesn't matter," she says. "If it's not from here, it doesn't belong here."

Of course, if you follow this logic to the end, then none of us hikers from the far side of the world belong in the Tasmanian wilderness either, since however lightly we tread, we're an alien species leaving an imprint. But this goes unsaid for the sake of diplomacy.

My bespectackled antagonist, Mary, and her sister are from Queensland. They do a backcountry trip together each year into the rain forests or Outback of Australia and have hiked everywhere imaginable. They're fierce about the "treading lightly on the land" ethic, to the point of packing out their poop. They've hooked up with Ted, an amateur boxer and nightclub bouncer from Melbourne who wears a jaunty digger hat, snapped up on one side like Bungalow Bill. Ted has lost his job and is at loose ends as to what he'll do next.

"I'm on the bum right now," he says, "camping around until I figure something out. I just pitch me tent wherever I can. Haven't paid for a campsite yet."

"Good on ya, mate." I can't resist trying to speak Australian.

Jeannette and I give a heave-ho to our mates and stumble into park headquarters a few hours later where we're revived with the help of colossal burgers and beers. A bloody leech wriggles on the floor beneath one table of backpackers in the shining, white, park cafeteria, a last remnant of the wild.

Minutes later, the wilderness is far behind as we board a bus for Hobart on the southern coast of Tasmania. The bus purrs out of the mountains and into a bucolic approximation of the English countryside as we roll past farmlands and small towns that have gone down-at-the-heels with a genteel poverty.

Land of Prisoners

"For you stole Trevelyen's corn,
So our babe might see the morn,
Now a prison ship is waiting on the bay."

- "The Fields of Athenry," *Irish ballad*

Hobart is one of the world's southernmost seaports. Further south is Port Arthur, one of the world's great museums of the macabre.

If you ever find yourself losing your mind in the solitary confinement cell of a maximum security prison, you can thank the 19th century prison authorities of Tasmania for your predicament. For it was at the Port Arthur prison camp that the model for the modern prison was created, with all its tortures of the body, mind and soul.

Australia was settled by convicts from the British empire, with the first of 162,000 petty criminals transported to Botany Bay, Sydney, via the First Fleet of 1788. Starting in 1830, an additional 73,000 people were sent to Van Dieman's Land (Tasmania). Typically, these "transports" were sentenced from 7 to 14 years for crimes such as stealing a handkerchief or a few turnips to save their starving children.

Author Robert Hughes, who wrote the convict history of Australia, "The Fatal Shore," said that being transported to Australia was considered as terrifying as being sent to Mars would be today.

Most convicts were loaned out by the government as farmhands or servants, but about one-seventh of them tried to escape or were repeat offenders for such crimes as poaching crayfish, getting drunk, or swearing at their masters. These could be sent to the harshest and most isolated prisons on Norfolk Island to the northeast of Australia, Macquarie Harbor on the west coast of Tasmania or Port Arthur. Men labored in the coal mines, dredged harbors in icy conditions, or cut timber, carrying the huge gum tree logs in a human centipede.

Port Arthur had a particularly cold, wet climate, and even young men who were in the prime of their youthful strength often died of exposure.

The recurring form of punishment here was flogging, in which a man would be chained to the "Iron Triangle" of three metal posts and given 100 lashes with a cat of nine tails. These were whips with leather knots stiffened by salt water which would literally rip the skin off a man's back. At Norfolk Island, where 300 lashes at a time were allowed, men were literally lashed to the bones of their rib cages.

But the lash failed to produce the obedience the British guards desired, since after a few whippings, a man's back turned to scar tissue devoid of feeling. It was the flogger and the prison authorities who suffered the humiliation of not being able to break a man, who became a hero to his convict mates for not crying out.

Then an English reformer came up with a less savage way of punishing convicts: constant surveillance, total isolation, and sensory deprivation through a new kind of prison which would serve as "a machine for grinding rogues into honest men." An incarceration machine which we still use today.

A "separate prison" was created at Port Arthur, in which prisoners were kept in solitary confinement to "reflect upon their crimes." They never saw another human face – except that of a hellfire-spouting preacher on Sunday services. Nor could they hear a word in their dark, soundproof cells.

When the prisoners were taken out for an hour of exercise each day, they were forced to wear hoods and turn their backs to the guards. Many went insane. The punishment of being driven mad by one's own solitary thoughts turned out to be far more effective than the lash or hard labor.

If that sounds like Guantanamo Bay or the Supermax prisons of America, it's because these techniques of mental torture were adopted by prisons around the world.

Like Auschwitz in Poland, a death camp that today resembles a pleasant college campus, Port Arthur is now a national park, filled with tourists who wander through its picturesque ruins. But like the former Nazi prison camp, you can't help but feel a brooding, somber mood beneath the historical displays and the shadows of human suffering.

Oz 2.0

Back on mainland Australia, a kangaroo melts out of the brush and slams into our car as we cruise along a country road by the sea. I get a sick feeling as we watch him writhing in the dirt in our rearview mirror. He flops around at the side of the road before lying still in what I assume is the death of him.

Poor, stupid kangaroo. What have we done?

The kangaroo looks like a large, malevolent brown mouse; a rather scary, man-sized mouse that hops around on hind legs flexed like truck springs, equipped with three-inch claws. But we don't want to see him dead. The seconds drag by as we watch him twitching on the pavement. Then, with a somersault twist, the 'roo flips sideways to its feet and bounds back into the bush.

"Oh no, our car!" Jeannette cries, leaping out the door to survey the damage.

"I can't believe it, not even a scratch," she says. "How is that possible?"

We peer at the fender, expecting it to be as crumpled as a white-tail deer collision back home in northern Michigan, but there's not even a dimple in the metal.

"He was going the same direction as us. He probably just bounced off the side of the car," I say. "Maybe he got off with a bruise and a headache."

"It's hard to say which would be worse, Australia losing another kangaroo or us banging a fender," Jeannette says.

We've landed back on the mainland where we've acquired the Ugliest Car in Australia in order to drive the classic Sydney-to-Cairns route. "Rolling Thunder" is the name we give to our elderly Ford Falcon station wagon.

Painted battleship gray, our ride is plastered with TRAVELLERS AUTO BARN in garish, orange, two-foot-high letters across the hood and sides, along with a four-foot diameter logo on the tailgate. Under the agreement we signed, we'd be on the hook for up to $2,700 if this tub gets banged up, even though it has more than 180,000 miles on the odometer.

"This thing looks like shit," I say a day after leaving the rental car lot. "Why didn't we demand another car when we had the chance?"

"Well at least the locals will know enough to steer clear of us in case we start driving down the wrong side of the road," Jeannette says.

Kangaroo collisions are one of the hazards of driving in Australia, and since they can hop along at speeds of better than 30 mph and are transfixed by headlights, they tend to get the job done when it comes to wrecking a vehicle. At the rental car place we signed an agreement not to drive at night when most bash-ups occur. Many vehicles in the Oz mount bull bars on their bumpers to bang away at kangaroos, which tend to leap out of nowhere at night.

The odd thing is that our collision took place at around 10 a.m. along a country road just north of Coffs Harbor, where we had spent the night camping just off the beach.

"Aren't kangaroos supposed to be snuggled up for a nap at this time of day?" Jeannette says. "I thought they were nocturnal."

"Maybe ours is a rebel. Or just not very smart."

Oddly, Sydney is the second largest city in the Oz but has no crosstown freeway on its north-south route. Thus, the traffic of half of Australia is forced to putz through town on a highway more suited to the 1940s.

It's agony creeping through town for two hours or so, but once free of Sydney's clutches we head for the wine country of Hunter Valley, continuing our quest to drink Australia dry.

Blessed with a sunny, grape-friendly climate, Australia produces oceans of wine, which is why the shelves of American stores are flooded with cheap Chardonnays from Down Under. There are hundreds of wine makers across the country and Jeannette and I have grown fond of shopping for a different bottle each night to share around our camp-site. Our daily toast in plastic wine glasses decorated with pictures of frolicking monkeys is the one expense we are cheerful to bear.

Hunter Valley also offers a huge concert venue in a vineyard where it just so happens that Sir Elton John is performing.

"One of my favorite albums in the '70s was 'Elton John in Austra-lia,'" I tell Jeannette over and over until her eyes glaze over. "It was a live double album with Elton playing along with an orchestra."

Starry-eyed with memories of that exquisite album, we plunk down in a chill rain to relish a concert I've been looking forward to for months. Alas, Sir Elton seems well past his shelf life with a stale show. He is possibly under the weather or fatigued from playing the same hits thousands of times.

"Well, how many times can someone play 'Crocodile Rock' without getting overdosed on it?" Jeannette says.

But we camp for free at a place called the Wollombi Tavern a few k's down the road. Apparently, many pubs offer free camping in Australia if you buy a meal and some beers.

It's a quintessential Aussie pub like you might see in a Crocodile Dundee film, full of grizzly characters and a motorcycle gang out rid-ing for the weekend. They're identical in every respect to the same species of biker you find in America: middle-aged, overweight and costumed in doorags, Harley-Davidson t-shirts and leather vests.

The bikers are gunning down a highway built over the Blue Moun-tains in the 1800s by convicts. For decades, the early settlers were stymied by the "impassable" Blue Mountains, unable to find a way over them. Finally, a trio of explorers bulled their way over the moun-tains, only to find, much to their surprise, cattle grazing on the other side. It turned out that stray cows had simply wandered around the southern end of the mountain range and found their way north.

It's hot driving up the coast, and getting hotter, since we are, in fact, heading closer to the Equator with each passing day. We're not inclined to turn on the air conditioning, since that would burn more expensive gasoline, which costs about twice as much as back in the States. So a hot, dry wind like a vented blast furnace funnels through the car all day as we lumber along at 60 mph.

The M-1 motorway linking Sydney with Cairns, 1,500 miles to the north, is not the joyride that the travel writers would have you believe. Thousands of trucks chug down this two-lane ribbon each day, playing chicken with frustrated motorists. No worries, mate, you just get used to angry blokes tailgating you all day long with monster semi-trucks whooshing inches from your windshield from the oncoming direction. It makes for a nerve-rattling, tight-ass drive under the glaring sun with a hot, dry wind blowing in your face from summer's oven.

Even the poorest state in America has a better freeway system than you'll find here, and many of the backroads are so narrow that they'd be considered bike paths back home. Yet the majority of the nation's 30 million people live along a narrow, east coast corridor.

"You'd think that a country that has trillions of dollars worth of mineral wealth would be able to come up with a better road than this," I grumble.

"Yeah, but then we'd just be driving too fast like everyone in America and we'd miss the sights," Jeannette says.

True, the slower pace of Highway 1 does incline one to make side trips. Some of the stops like Newcastle and Port Macquarie are uninspired blue collar factory & fishing towns, confirming my suspicion that Australia is a tropical Canada. But then come places like Byron Bay and Rainbow Beach, hippie-trippy scenes where the waves are necklaced with hundreds of surfers and the beaches packed with luscious girls in teeny bikinis.

The latter tend to remind me that our own libidos have been inhibited to a large extent by the problems of attempting to make love on an air mattress. Normally, Jeannette and I go at it like bunnies, but ironically, on this romantic camping trip of a lifetime I'm reluctant to do the deed for fear that our combined weight will pop one of our expensive air mattresses. And then where would we be? No, the long road to Cairns is not one of sexual ecstasy.

The surfers of Byron Bay may be having a better go of it, as they eschew tents in favor of sleeping in their cars and vans on the side streets around town. The doors of their rigs yawn open, revealing a surfer's swag of bedrolls and a grimy mess of camping gear, beer bottles and who knows? possibly some bikini bottoms.

"Can you imagine anyone camping in our neighborhoods back home?" Jeannette says, thinking of our uptight home town. "It would be front page news and people waving pitchforks."

On the Beach

It's rainy here at the northernmost end of New South Wales, pouring every night in the wet season. The rain drums for hours on our tent, never pitched more than a few hundred yards from the roaring ocean; quite a symphony, overall.

"Last year, 7,500 campers were trapped here on a beach campground without food, water or power when floods cut off the road for more than a week," a local tells us as we drive the coast south of Rainbow Beach. "Emergency measures were taken to bring in food and rescue the stranded campers."

"It's easy to see how people could get in a jam here pretty fast," Jeannette says as we bump along past scores of camping vehicles and tents jumbled every which way along an unregulated stretch of the coast. It looks like anarchy in paradise, without toilets, potable water or any store for miles around.

But, as the saying goes, "Life is a beach" when you're camping your way up the coast of Australia.

"I used to think that beachcombing would be a good alternative for people thinking of committing suicide," I say as Jeannette and I stroll into yet another sunset. "If life got too grim, you could just chuck it all and go live on a beach without any worries."

"You could look for seashells," Jeannette says, "or at least get in a good walk in the waves."

I speculate that beachcombing could have fixed the likes of Kurt Cobain, the grunge rocker who blew his brains out with a shotgun in 1994, or depression-prone author David Foster Wallace, who hanged himself in 2008.

But beachcombing is far too introspective a pastime to deter depressives from fatal thoughts. More likely, mellow thoughts on the beach are a poison, not a cure, for those who live too far up in their heads.

Yet there may be some value in travel as a therapy for holding onto one's sanity. Arthur Rimbaud famously ditched France and a career as the greatest poet of his time to become a wandering trader in the ancient Ethiopian city of Harar in 1880. "I sought voyages, to disperse enchantments that had colonized my mind," he wrote.

Jeannette and I walk for miles each day on a different beach as we creep up the coast: Coffs Harbour, Rainbow Beach, Fraser Island, Byron Bay, Mission Beach and more. I'd like to say we found a Great White washed up here and there, or a giant squid; perhaps the stump of Captain Ahab's leg, a Japanese bayonet or a message in a bottle from Henry Hudson.

But the only things of value we find are the swirling jewels of the sun going down on the sea in a chrysalis of neon red, purple and orange fire. That, and millions of mystifying patterns made by tiny crabs, spreading out along the sand as far as the eye can see.

We watch surfer dads teaching their 5-year-olds how to ride a board, or young dudes with dreads performing feats of derring-do among the rocks. Offshore, a stately procession of hundreds of container ships glides by far out on the horizon each day on their way around the world. It all serves to remind you what a tiny molecule you are in the makeup of the world.

Lost in the Ozone

"Put some sunscreen on!"

"Okay, okay!"

It turns out that beachcombing is a hazardous activity in Australia, owing to the thinning ozone layer. Jeannette and I foolishly stroll the sands each day in our bathing suits, sometimes without any sunblock on, while I notice that most of the Australians we see walking the beaches are covered up with clothing and hats, even in the sweltering sun.

The ozone hole threatening Australia is the result of man-made chlorofluorocarbons (CFCs) reacting with sunlight to create chlorine in the atmosphere. This in turn breaks down the protective ozone layer, which shields us from harmful, ultraviolet radiation. High-energy UV rays contribute to malignant melanoma.

Unlike the threat of global warming and climate change, where there seems to be nothing but knuckle-dragging going on to stop it, the discovery of a growing ozone hole above Antarctica in 1985 roused the governments of the world to near-immediate action.

Even Ronald Reagan signed the Montreal Protocol on Ozone Depleting Substances in 1988, a global decision to replace CFCs in aerosol cans, refrigerators and air conditioners with less harmful compounds.

Of course, these alternatives to CFCs were cheap to produce, so there was no economic incentive to gin up the sort of disinformation that's peddled by climate change deniers today. Perhaps if there had been huge sums at stake in the CFC industry, say, along the lines of today's coal industry, we'd all be wearing lead-lined suits by now and waiting for extinction.

Despite international action, the ozone layer remains notoriously thin over the South Pole in a "hole" that is particularly troublesome for Australia.

The First Australians

In the western world, Australia first made its appearance as a mythical continent. In the 1600s, European mapmakers theorized that there had to be a Great Southern Continent in the South Pacific to balance out the land mass of the northern continents. Turns out they were right.

Captain Cook first charted these shores in 1770, mapping the coast of eastern Australia. At that time, no one had a clue as to Australia's size; its shores had been touched on haphazardly here and there over the centuries by the 1521 Portuguese expedition of Christado de Mendonca, along with Dutch sailors out of Malaysia and traders from Indonesia. After Cook, not another soul from Britain showed up for the next 18 years until the First Fleet of 11 ships full of convicts set sail for Botany Bay in 1788.

On the shores of Rainbow Beach, Cook found sands colored in 72 shades by iron oxides, sparkling in diamond twinkles for as far as the eye can see. Nearby is Fraser Island, the largest sand island in the world, formed of china-white grains of silica.

"I thought every island was made out of sand," Jeannette says as we ramble around the island in a 40-passenger dune bus.

"No, islands are often covered with sand, but down below, they are rock formations pushed up from the sea by volcanic activity," our guide says. "Fraser Island is the only place on Earth that's entirely made of sand."

She tells us that for thousands of years, Fraser Island was inhabited by the Butchulla people, a band of Aborigines believed to have numbered from 400 to 600 people who made their living from the sea, harvesting fish and mollusks.

"During the winter when seafood was plentiful, they would invite other bands from the mainland over for month long parties of perhaps 2,000 people called corroborees. These festivals were meant to connect with the Dream Time."

"What exactly was the Dream Time?" I ask.

"It's a time when their ancestors arose from the myths of creation," she says. "It's the time when the spirits created human beings and the world we live in."

We ponder this information as our colossal dune buggy inches its way along the island roads past ancient trees, bristling with thorns, which might once have sheltered an Aborigine or two.

"The Dream Time can never be anything but a mystery to middle-aged tourists from the American Midwest," I decide. "Was it supposed to be another dimension? Or was it a metaphysical place up in the sky like heaven, full of invisible beings like our angels?"

"I don't believe in heaven," Jeannette says with a shrug.

"But do you believe in the Dream Time?"

"I wouldn't know unless I was an Aborigine living back then," she says. "And then, what choice would you have but to believe?"

Whatever the case, the Dream Time gave its children an excuse to party hearty. Imagine 2,000 people dancing naked on a beach of the purest white sand before a bonfire with flames shooting 30 feet high. All to the clacking of hundreds of rhythm sticks and the brontosaurus roar of an orchestra of didgeridoos. Their corroborees were said to have been orgiastic affairs filled with story-telling, drumming, dancing, feasting, ritual adornment and body painting that went on for weeks on end on the pearl-white island the Butchulla called K'gari, or "Paradise."

The Aborigines have the oldest surviving culture in the world, wounded and ruptured though it is today. They migrated to Australia somewhere between 50,000 and 80,000 years ago down the Malay Peninsula and across a land bridge which was drowned beneath the sea thousands of years ago. But since there were no domesticable plants or animals on the continent, beyond some dingos and giant sloths that were hunted to extinction, they never developed any sort of agriculture or civilization; instead, they lived as primitive hunter-gatherers for 50 millennia until the Europeans arrived.

They also dispensed with clothing, except for some paint for decoration or perhaps a layer of mud to deter bugs. Nor did they bother constructing homes, other than some rough huts. Australia has an abundance of heat and rock outcroppings, with little rain, so who needed garments or a roof?

But they did have a complex social structure, with rules of etiquette for everyone from married couples to proper behavior at their corroborees. They baked a form of bread from the nardoo plant and got high on the leaves of the corkwood tree. They knew the medicinal uses of many rain forest plants and had an artistic tradition of rock art, filling every corner of Australia with pictures of kangaroos, crocodiles, hunting exploits and unknowable spirits that are tens of thousands of years old. Many of these artworks have a strikingly modern aesthetic.

Grandmothers called the shots, choosing husbands for marriageable girls from "three skins away," meaning a separation of at least three cousins. Romeos who broke taboo against inbreeding risked a traditional punishment of a spear thrust through each leg.

And although they lacked the idea of private property, each man had "his" particular hunting area, the boundaries of which were marked by trees or rocks with spiritual powers.

It's claimed that their story-telling tradition passed down legends and deeds that happened thousands of years ago, back to the Dream Time when their ancestor spirits created the world. Even today, the elders of the Top End of Australia still tell the story of a battle with the crew of a Dutch ship that landed on this coast in 1640. By contrast, how many of us in the West know a thing about their ancestors from even two generations ago?

But the convicts, whalers and hard men who settled Australia couldn't see those traditions or simply didn't care. They seized Aborigine hunting grounds, cut down their sacred trees, and abducted girls for sex slaves or concubines. Convict settlers also grew to hate the Aborigines because they were enlisted by the authorities to hunt down and kill runaways from the penal colonies.

The Aborigines fought back. One ruse was to toss burning branches on a settler's roof at night, spearing the family members as they ran out the door. They also waylaid shepherds far out in the bush, who, as convicts had no choice but to be on a lonely watch, far from any hope of rescue.

Thus, the Aborigines became fair game for 150 years of extermination.

It wasn't all murder and mayhem; early explorers relied on the kindness of Aborigines for survival in the Outback. Nonetheless, Australian history is filled with stories of them being hunted for sport; given poison packaged as flour; even hunted for dog food. If you're looking for cruel stories, you'll find them in Australia.

Here on Fraser Island, the Aborigines were decimated by diseases and enslaved or murdered by Western sailors and miners. Most of the survivors were shipped off the island in 1904.

Troubles Back Home

"You'd better look at this," I say, handing our iPad to Jeannette at Rainbow Beach.

It's a disturbing email from back home. Our son, Nathan, and his wife, Nicole, who took up residence with their four kids in our house a few weeks before we left, announce that they're getting divorced. With the kids ages 6, 4, and 18-month-old twins, it's a disaster.

Nate has also suffered a crisis with his business partner and is suddenly both homeless and without a job. He's sleeping on a friend's couch, having been ordered by Nicole to leave our home, which we left him in charge of.

The next few weeks are filled with a flurry of email confessions and accusations, the more lengthy of which go unread. I send back perfunctory emails along the lines of "Glad to hear you two are working things out." Jeannette fires back with exhortations to "Keep communicating. Being able to talk about things is so important."

Heading up the coast, we stop at a McDonald's each day to avail ourselves of free wi-fi to hear the latest from the battlefield. But communicating over the web in rural Australia is iffy at best, and often we can't make a connection. Mickey D's wifi is also painfully slow and is disconnected every 20 minutes or so to discourage lingering.

"It's not that we don't care, but what else can we do when we're 14,000 miles away?" Jeannette says.

"I wouldn't care to be part of the drama even if we were home," I say.

"I hope they work things out."

"Yup."

Later we reflect that divorce, while painful, was the best thing that ever happened to us in our own prior marriages. Sometimes, it's best to move on.

As the weeks flow by, the emails slow to a trickle and Nathan and Nicole find their way down separate paths. But sharing four young children, they'll never be truly parted.

Camping Days

The thermometer continues to climb through the 90s as we head north. For the first time, we spend the night without our ponchos and sarongs piled on our thin, tropical sleeping bags to keep warm.

Our daily wakeup call is the orchestral cackling of birds.

"Some of them sound like barking dogs, others like baby lambs," Jeannette writes in our blog. "Then there's the screeching magpies... quite a racket, but you get used to it."

Mornings are spent over giant mugs of coffee and bowls of mangos and oranges ladled with passionfruit yogurt, usually with a spectacular view.

"My problem is that I like Australia so much that I'd like to move here every winter," Jeannette says over coffee one morning as we gaze upon a river feeding the sea at Moonee Beach.

"George Harrison moved here," I say hopefully, noting that The Beatles guitarist lived his final years on an island off Port Douglas.

"Even just camping here would be okay with me."

"Flying here every winter would be criminally expensive."

"Right, crazy idea. But I can dream, can't I?"

Australians are passionate campers, which they call caravanning. Every town has at least one caravan park, and often several right on the beach or within an easy stroll of the town center. Australia's roads are too narrow to accommodate the glut of monstrous road whales piloted by seniors in the U.S. Instead, the campgrounds here are packed with families camping in multi-room tents or pop-up trailers.

Camping is ragingly popular between Christmas and New Year's Day, when half of the country hits the road. It's said that many reserve next year's campsite the day after Christmas to make sure they've got a place to rendezvous with family and friends the following year.

We also see hordes of young people traveling everywhere in Australia. Hundreds of college-aged surfers and students are packed into hostels (called "backpackers" here) which occupy every beach town. Some of these hostels are landscaped resorts with swimming pools, bars, restaurants and game rooms. This, with 10 kids to a dorm who party their brains out until 5 a.m. at discos that run all night long.

We learn more about Australia as we crawl north along the coast:

• Australians really do say things like "cheers, g'day, crikey, cheeky monkey" and address each other as "mate." A chicken is a "chook," and if you're feeling sick you say you're "crook," as in "I'm crook from that bad chook, mate." And, even if you're hundreds of miles into the middle of the Outback without a hope of ever returning in the course of six lifetimes, the sales clerk is sure to say "See ya latah" with a laconic drawl as you leave her shop.

• Australia is the size of the continental United States, yet has only two seasons: wet and dry. One temperature seems to serve for both: hot and hotter, unless you're down to Tasmania where extra shivering is available.

• Australians have raised the lowly hamburger to an art form with a pile-up they call "the lot." This is a burger with beet relish, lettuce, tomato, carrots, ham, onion and an egg on a thick bun. Seven inches tall, it's designed more for the gape of a crocodile's mouth than our jaws.

Yet considering they cost double or triple what you'd pay in the U.S., burgers rarely seem to be all beef in Australia. They're more like meatloaf, adulterated with everything from lamb to rice, eggs and who knows what. But with a price as dear as Kobe steer.

• Australia's newspapers contain the most insipid prattle imaginable, with front page stories along the lines of "Firefighters Rescue Kitty from Tree!" in 3-inch headlines.

Things we consider to be minor "News of the Weird" items in America are pumped up as breathless dramas here, mostly involving families in crisis. Last week it was a dad using his acoustic guitar to beat off a saltwater croc that crawled into the family's living room. Elsewhere, a kitty-napper is on the loose - hide your cat! A couple's roof caves in; what in the world will they do? That sort of thing.

• And finally, don't ever get in the way of an Australian and his beer, mate.

See ya latah.

West of Brisbane, we visit Sharn and Kevin Duff, who reveal the challenges of running a ranch in Australia. We gun our beater station wagon high up a hill along a dirt track to their place which overlooks a broad valley. You can see perhaps 30 miles from their home, which opens up to an outdoor living space like a rustic villa.

Enthusiastic travelers whom I met several years ago in Vietnam, the Duffs travel as far as Asia and Europe each year. They don't live for the sake of travel, however; they own a spread of 600 acres in the heart of farm country where they raise 28 prime steers.

The Duffs are entirely dependent on rainfall for their water in a climate which gets dry as a dust broom for months of the year. They have nine large rain barrels on their property, each several times the size of a hot tub. Their property is also networked with ponds, called dams here, which are filled by rainwater flowing down from the roof of their home. The dams provide water and a cool bath for the steers.

Kevin points out parallel roads mowed through the grass down the hill from their home that serve as a firebreak during the dry spells.

"If a wildfire threatens, the grass between these roads is set on fire to create a firebreak," he says. "If the fire is really out of control, we can set a 40-acre parcel of woods on fire in advance of the firebreak to create an additional buffer."

"Doesn't that kill the trees?" Jeannette asks.

"The woods are filled with ironwood trees that are resistant to fire," Kevin says. "They don't suffer much damage if they're burned over."

The Coral Sea

With a cloudy day at hand, we do 12 hours in the car to make up for lost time, rolling along an inland route through miles of floodplains that stretch as flat as a card table to distant blue-gray mountains. The plains are dotted here and there with lone, towering gum trees and herds of brahma cattle, eerily beautiful in the distance.

"How are you holding up?" I ask. Jeannette is slumped against the passenger door, looking semi-comatose in the hot wind blowing through the car.

"I've never felt better in my life," she says.

"Seriously?"

"Seriously," she says with a dreamy look on her face and half-closed eyes. "We're alone together on the other side of the world, and no one back home has a clue about where we are or what we're doing. What could be better than that?"

Jeannette is less sunshiny that night when we stay in a run-down migrant workers' camp, filled with glum fruit pickers from China and Ghana, of all places. Arriving late in the evening in the rain without a chance to pitch our tent, we sleep in the dank, hot back of the station wagon, swatting mosquitoes through the night.

"Wake up, beauty queen," I call in the morning, videotaping my beloved's puffy face and toes in the cramped mess of the car.

"God, I feel grungy," she mumbles. "What a crappy place."

"Guess what? There's no shower here either."

Groan...

Nonetheless, driving through Queensland feels like freedom. The road ribbons its way through shadowy mountains and across pancake plains that spread across an area the size of France and Germany combined. Yet all this land was underwater just a few months before our arrival.

The sky looms over us like the face of God. Jeannette shares her feelings on our Hobo Highway blog: "I have seen a good many sunsets, one of my favorite things to witness, but never one like last night. Low, buffy black clouds, and I mean black, a streak of light blue, a little white, then some fiery, pinky stuff."

Fiery, pinky stuff - there seems to be a lot of that in Queensland.

At times we roll through dense clouds of smoke caused by burn-offs set by farmers. This is a backfire of acreage along the roadway to eliminate the chance of a much bigger wildfire rolling through, but it's a spooky feeling, driving through smoke as the evening settles in.

As the world's second driest continent after Antarctica, fire is just another aspect of the weather in Australia. Here are firestorms driven by winds of hurricane force with flames 300 feet high. The Aborigines terraformed Australia for tens of thousands of years with fire, using it to generate pastures of new shoots for game animals to feed on.

Edging deeper into Queensland, darkness falls after another day at the wheel and still no campsite to be found. We see kangaroos leaping through the brush just off the road and I recall our promise to the rental car company to never drive at night. The miles drift on as the darkness deepens, illuminated only by the hellish red of slow-burning fires along the road.

Then, rounding a curve, Jeannette spots a hand-lettered sign hanging from a tree, telling of a pub camping site. We roll into a rough-looking warren of beat-up trailers and a shack for a bar that is filled with coal miners on a fishing holiday. Their red skin is toned black with flecks of carbon and a there's a bit of a lost, anxious look about their eyes, as if wondering where they're going with their lives. A tough but vulnerable bunch.

A sign on the wall warns not to go in the ocean, for here dwells a small jellyfish whose sting is so excruciating that it stops the electrical connection to your heart. "If stung, keep giving the victim CPR, even if it appears he is dead," the sign advises. "Not all stings are fatal."

And there, just yards away, is the shore of the Coral Sea - a fabled place I've always wanted to see - where the U.S. Navy and its air force joined the Australian fleet for a pitched battle against the Japanese in May, 1942.

By one estimate, more than 106,000 U.S. sailors, marines and airmen died in the Pacific Theater of World War II. Hundreds still lie at the bottom of this sea, human bricks in the wall of ships and planes sent to fortify Australia and the Allied Command from attack by the Empire of Japan.

It was from this sea that the Western powers launched the counterattack, island-hopping their way 4,000 miles across the Pacific to the home isles of the Japanese.

In Another Land

As is so often the case when traveling, Jeannette and I are visiting two countries at the same time: Australia, of course, but also the Country of the Young, where we're as unexpected as space aliens.

With both of us approaching 60, we've reached the back yard of middle age together. Ahead lies the gate of old age, and though we haven't reached it yet, it's within sight. Hopefully, it's just a mirage.

In Airlie Beach we stay at a big hostel/resort camp called The Base where we pitch our tent, one of only three on the property; the kids are mostly holed up in dormitories or camper vans.

We're no strangers to the nightclub scene and feel at home that evening in the backpacker's patio bar, but everyone is 35-40 years younger than us, and I can't help feeling a bit like Ward Cleaver at sea among the young Beavers, Wallys and Eddy Haskels. The thump-thump-thump of dance pop goes on until 5 a.m., and the streets are packed with hundreds of excited kids on their way to the clubs.

"Everyone looks like they're going to the prom," Jeannette says.

"You'd better upgrade your wardrobe to keep up."

"Mmm."

A parade of young women passes by under the streetlights, tottering like cranes on five-inch heels, resplendent in skin-tight cocktail dresses, platinum-bangled sheaths akin to negligees, or poofy, tail-dragging gowns. The sartorial habits of the Australian male, however, are drab to the opposite extreme. The Ozzie men are uniformly dressed in cargo shorts and addicted to name-brand logo t-shirts: FILA, Billabong, Diesel or Converse, sometimes with sports team logos or the names of imaginary American universities.

They make for odd couples, she in her skyscraper heels and scrap of glittering party dress; he in his beer t-shirt and baggy shorts.

"Makes you feel old, don't it?" I say as the parade of youth dissolves into the night.

"I guess, but on the other hand, traveling makes me feel young," Jeannette says.

"That's my theory on the fountain of youth," I say. "Traveling and having lots of experiences allows you to live multiple lifetimes. Instead of trying to live to be 100 or 120, you're better off cramming several lives into the time you've got."

"So how old are you now?"

"I'm shooting for 150."

Setting Sail

Airlie Beach is the main port for cruising the Whitsunday Islands. This archipelago off the Great Barrier Reef was first spotted on the feast of the Sunday feast of the Pentacost in 1770 by Captain Cook. Today, a cruise of these islands is one of Australia's premier experiences.

We hook up with a boatload of 20-somethings for a three-day cruise on The Condor, which was the fastest maxi-class sailboat in the world from 1980-84. The mast alone weighs nine tons. Lining the rail like birds on a wire, we look down on a deck that appears to be almost straight down, with the sea ripping past the gunwales below. Occasionally, the bow dips into the waves, drenching those sitting up front.

One of the deckhands is Johnny, a young Chinese man from Hong Kong who gave up his job as an accountant to become a cabin boy on the boat. He reminds us of a backpacker we met in Tasmania: Adeline, a French woman with a master's degree who is working in the Australian hospitality industry while working her way around the world for three years.

Why would anyone give up a professional career in France or China to work a menial job in Australia? For Adeline it was adventure, perhaps. Fun. See the world – that sort of thing. Not so for Johnny.

"I wanted to move to Australia, and this was the only job I could find here," he says. He plans to pay his dues at menial jobs in Australia until he catches a break.

You can get a one-year working holiday visa in the Oz with an emphasis on casual employment. This is code for "doing the scut jobs that no Australian citizen wants to do." Initially, visa holders can't work at any single place for more than six months, but those who work for more than three months on a farm, fishery, plantation or in a mine are eligible for another year-long visa.

We're obliged to wear sting suits when we go snorkeling off the boat. These black long-johns are preventives against a jellyfish sting, including the nearly invisible Irukandji, which is the size of your baby fingernail and packs the most lethal venom on earth. Surviving its sting only means that you're so convulsed in pain that you wish you were dead. The captain tells us that failing to wear a suit could mean having to pay $7,000 for an emergency helicopter flight to the hospital and two weeks of treatment at $17,000 or more.

"What happens if you brush one with your hands or feet?" I ask.

The captain shrugs. "It's just the beginning of the jellyfish season, so hopefully, we won't run into any," he says. "The suits are only 75 percent effective in preventing a sting, anyway."

"How encouraging."

"These suits are better than sunscreen," Jeannette offers, looking like a Bond girl in hers. She keeps it on for most of the cruise.

The skulking jellyfish are why there are no surfers north of Airlie Beach, especially since the seas of northern Queensland also host giant crocodiles up to 18 feet long and Great White sharks that can measure 25 feet or so. The saltwater pools and swimming areas in the towns to the north are protected by nets of fine mesh.

Hmm... the captain failed to mention these hazards as we snorkeled and frolicked in the water off the boat.

A visit to Whitehaven Beach finds us in pure white sands as fine as talcum powder. Cited by National Geographic magazine as one of the three most beautiful beaches in the world, these sands are jealously guarded by the federal government. It's said that a few years ago, a tourist from Austria tried to take a small bottle full of sand out of the country and was fined $52,000 for his indiscretion. He remained in jail until he could mortgage his home to pay the fine. This strikes me as an urban legend, but it makes for a good story.

Once again, we are surprised to find that we are at least 30 years older than anyone else on the boat, more like 35 years, actually. Whatever happened to our generation? The generation of sex, drugs and rock & roll? Parked in La-Z-Boys somewhere and hooked up to urine bags and the Home Shopping Network, no doubt.

No worries - Jeannette and I have a blast, partying 'til dawn with wild abandon, manic dancing, puking off the deck, drunken debauchery and lusty yells, embarrassing the younger generation with our reckless behavior. Well, not really. I'm one of the first to go beddy-bye in an airless berth that's tighter than a coffin after drinking some funky boxed wine called "goon." Jeannette at least stayed up late and slept on deck a bit, so cheers to her for maintaining our honor.

Mating Rituals

Although I try not to notice, the journalist in me can't help but observe that there are a number of very good-looking women in their 20s lolling around the deck in their bikinis for the entire cruise. Being a young hottie isn't what it used to be, however.

"Guys are wimps. They just don't want to ask you out," a voluptuous brunette from Canada tells us. "They just send you a text, or want you to hang out with their friends. There's no date, no romance, just pizza and beer."

"They don't want to commit," says her friend from Brisbane. "You're going along, thinking everything is great and then, poof! They're gone, like it was just nothing. Two years I was with this guy, then, gone."

This, they say, is the age of the college-style group date, where a mob of friends connect to socialize, and if two of them manage to hook up later in the evening, cool. It gets the job done, but without the fireworks.

Two young guys, software designers from New Zealand, nod their heads in unsympathetic agreement. "Yeah, that's the way it is," one says, anxious to get back to texting on his phone. "It's much easier to just send someone a text."

Personally, I doubt that texting a hot woman with an invite to come over and knock boots over microbrews after midnight works all that well for most men.

But gone are the days of dating where a man screwed up the courage to ask a woman out via a tortured phone call, arrived with a bouquet of flowers, opened the car door and squired her around to dinner and a show, picking up the tab and hoping for a kiss instead of a hug at the end of the night if things went okay - often, not the case.

God that could be painful. Dating was a vestige of chivalry invented by the white middle class. It required social skills, strategy, timing, luck and courage. Not to mention a sense of humor and a hide well-suited for rejection. Maybe younger guys are onto something with their wimpy texting and herd dates.

Dig this: Rudolf the Rednosed Reindeer was spotted in Airlie Beach when we got off the boat! He's the bloke who stupidly took along #4 sunscreen for a three-day sail under the tropical sun when #50 was called for.

Bugs & bats for Christmas

With Christmas only a few days away, Jeannette and I fear we'll be stuck sleeping in the back of our station wagon for the error of not having booked a campground months in advance.

It turns out the warnings about crowded campsites are bullshit, but it prompts us to book five days at a garden campground on Magnetic Island. Located just shy of Townsville, the island got its name from Captain Cook, whose compass went a bit crazy here in 1770.

Magnetic Island turns out to be kind of a bummer. The Bungalow

Bay Koala Camp serves as a preserve for the teddy bears and there are flocks of lorikeets here, along with a mini zoo of crocodiles, possums and many birds. It's a lovely place, but hundreds of giant flies make our stay miserable. The insect equivalent of flying trucks, these pests are about an inch in diameter, buzzing around our heads constantly. They don't bite, but they settle on your skin, presumably to drink your sweat, and make each outdoor meal a nauseating experience.

In addition to the flies, Magnetic Island steams like a tropical furnace. We're absolutely drenched in sunscreen, sweat and bug repellent all day long, alleviated only by pitchers of beer at night. Drenched in gook at Christmas, of all times.

At dusk, flying foxes the size of small dogs glide overhead as we make our way to grill some chook on the barbies at the beach, a place the flies avoid.

With the Christmas week temperatures near 100 degrees Fahrenheit, we spend most of our time on the island hiking its harsh hills (mindful of death adders) or reading books in the shallow end of the camp's pool.

"I like reading in the pool," Jeannette says, clutching a damp copy of *U Is for Undertow* by Sue Grafton. "Seems like we're setting a record for it."

"There are worse things to do with our time," I agree, poring over *Half Past Midnight.*

Indeed, a long backpacking trip brings out the reader in you, and like a sugar addict, you start craving the sweet junk food side of literature. We raid the book exchanges of every hostel, campground and laundromat we come across, consuming the romantic thrillers of Sydney Sheldon and the tough guy prose of Frederick Forsyth. We tear through dozens of books, leaving behind such treasures as *Shantaram* by Gregory David Roberts, *The Lost City of Z* by David Grann and *Drop City* by T.C. Boyle.

One night, while suffocating in the heat and lying naked atop our sleeping bags, we find people peering in our tent, followed by a stick thrown at us. We're under attack! I'm furious, vowing to beat the crap out of these motherfuckers, charging around in the dark looking for them with an anxious Jeannette in tow.

But it turns out to be a gang of bored 14 and 15-year-olds from town who resent tourists infringing on their stultifying paradise. A night-long skirmish with a bunch of kids sounds like a no-win situation, so I call it quits on any crap-beating. Soon they melt back into town.

But all is not lost: sitting before our plastic Christmas tree from a dollar store, we reflect on how strange the holiday seems in a land without snow.

"There's something about a plastic Santa Claus standing next to a palm tree in the blazing sun that doesn't seem right," Jeannette says.

"The Australians don't knock themselves silly over Christmas the way we do in the U.S.," I say. "They play Christmas music in town and have big sales, but it doesn't seem like they spend themselves into the poorhouse on presents."

"Maybe it's because Christmas falls in the summer here when it's more like our Fourth of July," Jeannette says. "Who wants to go shopping when you'd rather be surfing?"

"Strangely, I don't miss spending hundreds of dollars on Christmas this year."

So, like our non-Thanksgiving, Christmas in the Oz is kind of a bust. I whip up an inedible pasta meal which is memorable only for its wretchedness. Who knew that Australian spaghetti sauce was so horrible? And between our budget and a desire to travel light, we have no gifts to give each other.

But we have each other on the far side of the world, and a three-dollar plastic Christmas tree. We splurge on renting a small hut at the campground, and snuggling within its walls, it seems like enough.

Welcome to the Wet Tropics

Free of Magnetic Island and the ritual of Christmas, we move on through Townsend, a sweltering town by the sea which serves as the gateway to the north. A sign up the road on the way into the burg of Mission Beach informs us that we've arrived in the "Wet Tropics."

Sure enough, we are continually wet with rivulets of sweat and clutching at the slightest chance for a bit of shade or the cooling puff of an ocean breeze.

The temps are in the 90s here, with high humidity, and Mission Beach is still vibrant with the memory of cyclones Larry and Yasi, which trashed the coast in 2006 and 2011. Since we'll be living in this range of temperatures for the next five months, we're acclimating to the idea of walking around for the duration of our trip in soggy clothes and hand-washing what we need each day.

"No need for an electric dryer here," Jeannette says, draping her blouse over a tent line.

"Ha-ha!"

Fortunately, this is the rainy season, so there are cooling clouds every day, and hours of light rain at night.

Tiny critters and creepy-crawlers seem to love the wet tropics. Millions of tiny crabs work the beach, turning the hard-packed sand into a vast mosaic of sand pebbles that serve as a shag carpet for one's toes.

Last night we watched TV for the first time in a month at an open-air camp pavilion. Dozens of toads, some as big as my fist, roamed the floor, chasing down bugs with a hop and a gulp. Beetles as long as two inches skittered between them, and on the ceiling, various lizards and geckos walked upside down on suction-cupped pads.

Today's expedition is in search of the wild cassowary, a four-foot-tall flightless bird with a bony, rainbow-hued crown which lives in the forests along this coast. The cassowary is a 15 million year-old relic of Gondwanaland, the ancient supercontinent which split apart ever so long ago to form the seven continents we know today. Australia drifted off 50 million years ago and its animals developed an evolutionary stream that was independent of the rest of the world.

At night we hear a tremendous racket outside the tent and imagine it's a dust-up involving these warlike birds. It's not worth the bother of getting up, however, since we hear much the same from all the other rainforest birds each morning: screeching, whistling and barking as if to warn of a 5-alarm fire.

Australia is a bird-lovers paradise, better even than Costa Rica.

The kookaburra, for instance, is a breed of kingfisher that eats bugs and worms in addition to fish, employing a black, three-inch beak as solid as a tack hammer which anchors its beige and brown body. Many times we've watched these grim-faced hunters perched in a tree, diving into the foliage below for a bug to gobble. For a bird noted for such a lusty laugh, these kooks sure affect a sour expression.

"I imagine there must be so many birds here because there are so many tasty bugs for them to eat," I say.

"This is a bug paradise," Jeannette agrees. "Thank God we've got all these birds around or they'd carry us away. You, especially."

Next to Jeannette, my best friend in Australia is a can of bug spray, which I employ with passion at the first hint of dusk. This is because I have the flavor of cocaine and ice cream to biting insects, while Jeannette seems to go untasted.

Along with giant toads, bugs and birds, Mission Beach teems with so many German tourists that it might serve as a tropical Saxony. We've encountered so many Germans at every turn in Australia that I can't imagine there are any of them left back in Stuttgart or Hamburg if they're scattered in a similar ratio all over the world.

Also strange, at a bar in Mission beach we hear an entire 1971 album by Detroit rocker Bob Seger on the jukebox, including some obscure tunes I haven't heard since, well, 1971. You'd be unlikely to hear these old songs ever again in the Motor City itself, yet here they are on the far side of the world.

One of America's greatest exports is music and curiously, every bar band in the world seems to cover "Sweet Home Alabama," written more than 40 years ago by redneck rockers Lynyrd Skynyrd. The song was written as a disgruntled response to Neil Young's blast at southern racism. It includes references to Watergate and stands tall for then-governor George Wallace, who was a standard-bearer for segregation. What can this decrepit song mean to Australians, and to the Thais and Indonesians we'll hear playing it down the road?

Cairns at Last

We roll into Cairns on Jeannette's birthday in late December, wrapping up one of the world's great road trips. Cairns is a jump-off for visitors to the Great Barrier Reef and the last big city on the way north on this end of the Oz. This is the end of the rainbow for tens of thousands of tourists who make the trek 1,500 miles up the coast from Sydney.

That night, we celebrate Jeannette finally getting all growed-up with a fat camp candle on top of our last piece of fruitcake. A chorus of "Happy Birthday" wafts through the sea breeze on our hostel patio.

"It took us nearly a month to get to Cairns, but we could have easily spent two," she says, noting that we passed up dozens of beaches, parks and small towns on the way north.

"We won't see them in this life, at least," I say. "You could spend years here and not see it all."

That seems to be especially true of native Australians. We've met many young Ozzies who have traveled all over the world, yet have never seen much of their own country. They plan to save poking around the Oz for their old age, doing what they call the "gray nomad" thing.

Rolling into town, Cairns looks like a tropical Anchorage, a horror of urban sprawl that goes on for miles in a glut of auto lots, motels and pre-fab metal buildings. Fortunately, the town center has a pleasant mix of restaurants, shops and a night market. Cairns also sports a large saltwater swimming lagoon, protected by a net to deter jellyfish, sharks and crocodiles.

By luck, we arrive practically at the door of a YHA hostel in the heart of town. The hostel is a virtual palace after weeks of camping; it's laid out hacienda style with a large courtyard filled with palm trees, a pool, outdoor dining area and the usual shared kitchen.

For once, Asian backpackers outnumber the Germans. We hear them exchanging information on where they're from: Korea, Vietnam, China. They're a quiet bunch, in general, and as the saying goes, birds of a feather.

"I'm going to miss camping," says Jeannette. "It's like we're losing our home, sweet home."

"Me too. Staying in hostels and cheap hotels brings you down after awhile," I note. "But we don't have any choice if we're heading on to Asia. They don't have a clue about camping up that way."

Later, we decide to go to a movie to get out of the heat, only to discover that a trip to the flicks runs $18 in Australia, more than twice the price of a show in the U.S.

"There's no way we can afford that," Jeannette says sadly as we turn away from the theater. "How are we doing on money, anyway?"

"We've blown nearly 40 percent of our budget. We can't get out of Australia fast enough, the way it's going."

"Won't it cost a lot to stay in hotels in Asia?" Jeannette wonders.

"Believe it or not, it will cost less to stay at an upscale hotel in India than what we spend on a campsite or a hostel in Australia."

On the plus side, we've each lost at least 10 pounds as a result of splitting lunches and opting for dinners that emphasize salads and cookouts in order to save money.

Jeannette is thrilled to have slimmed down.

"We blend in better with the skinny bunch at the hostel," she says.

"Yeah, and we want to be thin by the time we reach Indonesia and India," I say. "We don't want look like typical blimpy Americans, even though I'm sure we'll still appear that way to Asians."

At the hostel, we endure the braying of a drunken Aussie jackass in the courtyard below for a couple of nights on end, blubbering in his beer. It makes us think of how much we miss the womanly scream and hiss of the kerloo bird outside our tent each night.

The River of Bats

On our last night in Cairns we watch a stream of thousands of bats flying overhead as we dine by the harbor. With a wingspan of three feet or so and poised as stiff as ballerinas, the flying foxes careen down the avenue above the outdoor cafe where we're sitting, some flying as low as the street lights. Beautiful in their grace.

The Saturday night crowd gapes from below. How many bats? It seems like somewhere between 5,000 and 10,000. It's tough to say, but the river of bats streams overhead for more than half an hour as darkness falls, heading for the mountains across the bay under a full moon.

Later we learn that this colony of spectacled flying foxes is both a tourist attraction and a matter of concern in the central business district. According to a 2012 report by the Cairns Regional Council, the colony living in the forest outside of Cairns contains an estimated 15,000 to 20,000 bats.

It makes for a meal with an unforgettable dinner show. For the record, we had a tandoori chicken pizza with red pepper and almonds, a green salad, and a bottle of Sauvignon Blanc. Fortunately, no bat shit garnish.

The End of the Road

Our tires hit the gravel at Cape Tribulation in Queensland's far north and the absolute end of the paved road in Australia.

We've done it! Wandering a spaghetti route of 3,000 miles all told, from Port Fairy to Cairns, with Tasmania to boot.

Beyond this, it's dirt road all the way to Van Arnem's Land in the Top

End, where 4-wheel-drive and an elevated exhaust muffler are essential because much of the road is underwater during the rainy season.

We spend the night at a camp on the beach just south of Cape Tribulation in the Daintree Rainforest. The Daintree is 200 million years old, the oldest rainforest in the world. It's 20 times older than the Amazon, an impenetrable tangle of trees and jungle creeping up the mist-shrouded mountains from the sea. It's one of the "tops" on the list of any visit to Australia; unfolding like a biological cathedral as we creep along a narrow road carved into the side of Mount Alexandra and roll slowly and reverently through an endless tunnel of trees.

"Oh my God, look!" Jeannette points.

We spot a beauty of a cassowary crossing the road, bobbing slowly and majestically with its crown of bone, rainbow head and furry feathers. It's perhaps five feet tall.

There are few trails in the Daintree; it's simply too wild, enmeshed in a riot of stinging vegetation that grips and pricks with every step. But Jeannette and I find a 2.7k trail, "for adventurous hikers only," and plunge into the forest, following a faint trail marked only by shreds of plastic ribbons. I walk headlong into the web of a 3-inch spider.

"Wouldn't want to get lost out here," says Jeannette.

"No shit!" I respond, waving a stick before me on the trail to ward off any lurking monsters. "How did the Aborigines ever find their way around?"

Later, we walk in a light rain along the beach to Cape Tribulation, a mile from our campsite.

"I can't believe we're really here," I gush, overwhelmed as we gaze at the headlands through the haze of the sea. "This is a place I've always wanted to visit."

That's because I love the stories of circumnavigators, and it was on this very spot in 1770 that Captain James Cook's ship, the Endeavor, struck a coral outcrop of the Great Barrier Reef and was hulled. The crew faced the threat of being sunk or marooned on the far side of the world. Cook limped into a river north of here at the present site of Cooktown and winched his ship ashore, spending more than six weeks repairing it.

For these men, it must have been like being stranded on Jupiter. Yet, small world today, our campsite neighbors are a family of three from Moscow.

"We're camping all the way to Sydney," says the father, who speaks good English and says he's an officer in the Russian army. I imagine he must be a general to afford such a trip. He and his wife have a small son, about eight years old, and they're traveling in a tidy camper van.

"My son studies English at a special school in Moscow," his dad says proudly, asking his son to demonstrate a few words.

We are suitably impressed. What a marvel that old Cold War enemies are met at the far end of Australia, of all places, enjoying the grace and understanding that travel brings.

Not far from our campsite, in a bleak mood over the wreck of his ship, Cook named Cape Tribulation and nearby Mount Sorrow after his state of mind; and who can blame him? He was the first of many mariners to get trapped within the 1,200-mile reef, many of who sank to the bottom of the sea without ever finding their way out.

Cook went on to claim this continent as New South Wales for King George III. We claim only the thrill of having completed 3,000 miles across Australia, with more to come.

The Top End

One of the hazards of traveling is hyperbole. Scary stories of what's ahead keep millions of us (billions?) at home.

I, for instance, expect to be engulfed in terrifying sheets of lightning as we complete the 1,000-mile flight to Darwin across a corner of the Outback, the Gulf of Carpentaria, and the vast swamplands of Kakadu National Park.

All through our trip, Australians have warned us to avoid Darwin during the rainy season. "Oh, you're not going there in January, are you? Oh, no, no, no."

They speak of endless sheets of rain and a blanket of wet heat that requires you to drink buckets of water just to maintain.

I've also read that Darwin is home to some of the fiercest electrical storms on earth, with skeins of lightning that paint the sky from one horizon to the other. The Aborigines here recognize six seasons through the year and this is Gudjewg, height of the wet season and the time of violent thunderstorms. At midnight on Christmas Eve, 1974, the entire town was smashed flat by Cyclone Tracy.

"Unfortunately, when you're traveling around the world, you can't always pick and choose the weather everywhere you go," I say to Jeannette during our flight after giving her a rundown on what's ahead. "If we want to see the Top End, we're stuck with the weather."

"It seems like we're always going someplace at the 'wrong' time of year anyway," she says. "We can handle it."

This is true. We once went to Hong Kong in the inferno of August at the height of the SARS epidemic because round-trip airfares from the U.S. were only $600 and hotels hit rock-bottom rates. We stayed at the same five-star hotel frequented by the likes of Frank Sinatra, Madonna, a pope and a U.S. president at a fraction of the usual price.

Yet, given all the warnings, I expect our plane will endure a terrifying landing in a lake on the runway, if we survive the legendary lightning of the Top End.

But there isn't a cloud in the sky as we touch down, and Darwin has a pleasant, spanking new appearance as a result of being completely rebuilt not so long ago. We stash our gear in a hostel downtown and set out to explore the town.

"I guess you've just got to go and see for yourself when you hear bad things about a place you're visiting," Jeannette says as we wander through a deserted park, wary of the occasional weaving drunk.

"Yes, so it seems," I say. "Though in this heat, tourists are as rare as eskimos."

Darwin was infamous for its fights and public drunkenness just a few years back and still has a bit of a rough reputation. With a handful of street people wandering around, the otherwise empty park has a spooky vibe and seems an ideal place to get bushwhacked. It looks like a scene from the '60s zombie flick, "Night of the Living Dead."

Jeannette is notoriously squeamish about cinematic violence, often running from the room whenever we watch the sort of blood-soaked videos that are standard fare in America. The iffy characters in the park make me wonder how she'll react if we're ever in a situation where we need to defend ourselves.

It's the sort of thing that crosses your mind when you're traveling around the world, in and out of dodgy situations. And of course, I wonder how I might react myself, since even a boxer has no control over which way his nerves will go in a fight-or-flight situation. Who knows if a confrontation will turn me into a quivering jellyfish or a crouching tiger? Or both, from moment to moment? That's why teachers of the martial arts emphasize mental control to as great a degree as actual fighting.

But we survive our walk around the lonely part of town undisturbed, and as it turns out, there was some sort of Giuliani-style crackdown in Darwin a few years back to clean up the place.

Evidence of this is apparent when we try to purchase a bottle of wine and get "carded."

"Oooh, I love getting carded," Jeannette says, thinking the clerk has mistaken her as someone under the legal drinking age.

"It's to see if you're on the banned drinking list," the clerk responds dryly.

"You ban people from drinking?"

"Yes, people who have problems with alcohol," he says with a grimace.

Local Aborigines on the dole are the chief targets of the town's Banned Drinker Register, having much the same problem with alcohol as the ruined communities of Native Americans.

Later, we see several middle-aged Aborigine women collecting welfare payments from a social services center before making a beeline to a nearby liquor counter. Whether they use the booze for trade or simply to keep their men happy we don't know, but it seems obvious the Banned Drinker Register isn't working all that well.

Going to Extremes

The Top End offers three major parks evoking Australia at its raw best, with Litchfield National Park being the most hospitable, a short drive south of Darwin. We spend a couple of days camping in the park, renowned for its waterfalls and swimming holes.

We're surprised to find that one of Litchfield's most famous bathing spots is closed because a saltwater crocodile has been spotted in the area, putting the oasis off limits. It has migrated upriver from the sea and there may be others.

But nearby, we manage to plunge beneath the spray of Florence Waterfall at a swimming hole in the forest. It's the closest thing I've had to a spiritual experience in years. The thundering cascade; the sun splashing diamond-bright off the crest of the falls; the cavelike recess behind the curtain of falling water. I feel drawn to the heart of nature's expression of God. My sunglasses catch the glint of what appears to be a mosaic of blue opals reflecting like neon tetras on either side of the falls. Very LSD. I tow Jeannette to the base of the falls and we tread water, holding hands beneath its thunder.

From Litchfield the road heads south across the length of Australia, bisected by Ayers Rock, nearly 1,200 miles to the south. The massive butte rising from the desert of the Outback is a symbol of Australia, displayed on souvenir knick-knacks everywhere you go in the country, but we have neither the heart nor the time for the 20-hour drive there, not to mention getting back.

A place of extremes, the Top End is home to many of Australia's 150,000 Aborigines, who are locked in their own extreme struggle for their future. We see evidence of their ruin everywhere, along with some hopeful signs.

Today, the Aborigines are trying to pick up the pieces of their shattered world, many of whom are living on the dole and coping with substance abuse, gangs and domestic violence. You see a lot of feel-good government propaganda all around the country, including posters and pamphlets claiming that the Aborigines are on the rebound, reclaiming their traditions and moving forward. But it all rings a bit hollow when we see bands of men standing idle on street corners or catch the gagging odor of women who haven't bathed in weeks.

This welfare society is the post-genocidal burden of white Australia, which hasn't sussed a way out of the legacy of the past (hint: provide some jobs). The Aborigines seem to be invisible to the whites here, and vice-versa, with little, if any, communication between the races. It's as if we occupy separate dimensions.

Several days later, we see bands of Aborigines sitting beneath the shade of trees across from a shopping mall in the town of Katherine, far to the south of Darwin. They huddle cross-legged on the ground against the hammer of the sun.

"They must sit there all day long every day for years on end," I say. "What a life."

"But that's what they've probably been doing for thousands of years to avoid the heat," Jeannette says. "They're probably talking about their families and friends."

"That would be the world's longest running soap opera."

"But it beats walking around in the hot sun all day."

Point scored. Without jobs or a cultural heritage that includes the concept of work; without the lost skills of the hunt and living in the bush; without the milder climate of the distant past, what else is there for a destitute Aborigine to do?

Yet, the Aborigines have nowhere else to go but up. Traditional ways are being reintroduced in their tribal homelands, and there's a growing middle class of those who work for the parks or in the tourist business. In some ways they are looking to the past to find their future.

Prisoners of the Sun

"What's that?" Jeannette sits up in the darkness of our tent, which is pitched in an empty campground at Katherine Gorge.

"I don't know." We lie silent, holding our breath, our ears straining at the darkness.

Something is bumping around our tent that's too big to be a toad or a bird and too small to be a person. Plus, it's jet black outside and a prowling maniac wouldn't be able to see a thing without a flashlight. I'm dying of thirst and head out for a drink of water at midnight to find a tiny kangaroo on the path, about three feet tall. Cute little feller, he lets me get within petting distance of him. Others appear in my headlamp, their eyes glowing in the glare.

We enjoy hearing the thump-thump-thump of a small mob hopping through the campgrounds for the rest of the night, finding more than a dozen here by morning.

Katherine Gorge lies about 200 miles south of Darwin. It was surrealistic driving there down a long empty highway in the blasting sun. Occasionally a road-train went by in the other direction, with a monster semi pulling three or four truck trailers at 70-80 mph.

The gorge reminds us of Lake Powell in the Utah desert, an oasis of water canyons. A natural oven, the gorge proves far too hot to go hiking as we had planned; it's perhaps 115 degrees or more. We are prisoners of the sun, reading in the campground pool amid a swarm of giant wasps, which buzz back and forth over our heads.

"Kind of tough on a couple of action monkeys like us," I say.

"Who'd ever imagine that we'd turn down going for a hike?" Jeannette responds. "Nothing ever stops us."

"We're getting soft."

Defeated by the heat, we take a boat ride through canyons 300-400 feet high and view rock paintings that are 8,000 to 15,000 years old.

"This painting is of a Mimmi ancestor spirit," says Gerry, an Aborigine who serves as a guide to the canyon. He points out an otherworldly painting of a spiny, red being surrounded by frolicking kangaroos and other animals.

"The paintings told visitors what kind of game they could find here when they were passing through," Gerry says. The drawings are expressive in a whimsical way, like fine art cartoons, and there are two small handprints on the canyon wall.

"The painting has been signed by the artist with his hands," Gerry says, "perhaps 10,000 years ago."

Dark as a starling, even under the full sun, Gerry has a shoulder-length cascade of blue-black curls falling to his neatly pressed ranger shirt. He has an easy smile, which lights up his face like a crescent moon.

"Is being a park ranger a good job?" Jeannette asks.

"Oh yes," he says. "Mostly."

Gerry explains that jobs for Aborigines tend to be limited to manual labor or working as farmhands or cowboys. A lucky few work as rangers or guides in the parks.

"If you want to see people living by the old ways you have to go out to the islands," he says, referring to a smattering of tribal refuges located off the coast of the Top End. Here, the ancient ways are still practiced, largely for the benefit of tour groups, but also at the urging of elders seeking to preserve the almost-lost traditions.

But mingling with the Aborigines of Bathurst or the South Goulburn Islands comes with a crushing expense, too high for our backpacking budget. That, and tours have vanished with the season.

In Kakadu

Moving on, our tiny red rental car buzzes on like a beetle through the furnace of Kakadu National Park, the "big one" in the Top End. The thermometer is pushing past 100 degrees.

"You know, I think this car must be running on three cylinders," I say. "I've got the pedal to the floor and it doesn't make a lick of difference."

"Maybe it's only got three cylinders and we're running on two of them. Let's hope we don't get stuck out here," Jeannette says, gazing out on a semi-desert of bugs and thorns shimmering in the heat. This is combined with the kind of humidity you associate with sticking your head in a laundromat dryer.

We have virtually the entire 12,000-square-mile park to ourselves as we hum down its back roads with the air conditioning running full blast with no effect. The size of many small countries, Kakadu is owned by the Aborigines. It's fearsome in its scope; a land of rain forests, swamps, canyons and rivers, known for its salt-water crocodiles which range up to 20 feet in length.

A solitary hike through the bush leads us to a 20,000-year-old rock shelter in the wilderness. We stop to admire the many cave paintings of kangaroos, turtles, lightning spirits, dancers and hunters, and imagine a time thousands of years ago when the laughter of children echoed through these painted halls of stone. There are 5,000 rock art sites in Kakadu alone.

Looking out from the heights of this cave, we gaze out across the endless bush, the fire-scorched trees, swamps and a faraway escarpment tearing a seam in the earth and try to see it through the eyes of ghosts long gone.

I imagine myself as an Aborigine 20,000 years ago. Black as a moonless night, lean as a sycamore tree, naked except for a bamboo spear. The plain below would have teemed with wallabies, easy game and edible plants.

Thousands of years ago, it's believed that the climate around Kakadu National Park was much milder than it is today, a paradise for those who lived in this soaring cave. But for us, it's an inferno of heat and biting insects.

"I'm glad we have our bug hats on," Jeannette says from behind a veil of netting. Even in this heat we're covered from heat to toe.

There's no swimming allowed in Kakadu, but a few years back some college kids ignored the warning; a 20-year-old woman was seized by a saltie and dragged under, never to be seen again. Underwater, the crocodile goes into a death spiral until its prey drowns. Then it tucks the carcass under a log until it is nicely rotted for good eating.

We wander on through the park, finding the roads and campgrounds virtually deserted; only a couple of clueless dopes from northern Michigan would show up during the hottest time of the year.

That night we hide out in our tent to escape a blizzard of biting flies and watch the film, "Purple Rain," on the iPad, headphones turned way up. Afterward, rivers of sweat run down our bodies as we lay naked on our mattresses. It's perhaps 90 degrees on an airless night.

"It's like our own private sweat lodge in here," Jeannette says to the darkness.

"It's getting ready to rain."

"Bring it on."

Despite misgivings about the infamous rainy season, I had hoped to see the spectacular storms that flood highways and rain day and night. But it has been freakishly dry this season in the Top End, a topic of local concern.

Yet later that night the rain came, bringing the crack of the thunder god's voice. One lightning strike shivers near our tent, loud as an artillery shell.

"Good way to put your buns in a knot," Jeannette murmurs.

"Ya," I say, peering into the darkness where the lightning skips and hops like aboriginal spirits across the Outback.

Alas, that was our last night of camping. Returning to a hostel in Darwin, we give away our beloved tent, camp chairs, duffel bag and other gear, all of which are too heavy to mail home. We've got only our backpacks to carry on with now, along with my mini guitar.

"It feels like we're giving away some old friends," Jeannette says as our tent disappears. One by one, patrons of the hostel pick at our giveaways until everything that has served as our traveling home is gone.

Down at the harbor, we look to the northwest across the Timor Sea towards Indonesia. After two-and-a-half months of camping our way across the Oz, we're heading for the Muslim lands of southeast Asia.

Indonesia

With her black poncho on and a black rainfly covering her back-pack, Jeannette looks like a giant licorice jelly bean wading knee-deep through the waters of Kuta, the gateway to Bali.

A jellybean with legs, a straw hat, and an ear-to-ear smile.

"How long do you think it will rain?" I had asked a young cook at breakfast.

"Maybe until tonight. Maybe all week," he said.

Not good, since a wall of water has poured from the sky since 4 a.m., keeping us awake with a thunderous drumming on the roof.

We've been in Kuta for five long days and are anxious to be on our way. Checking out of our hotel, we wonder where all of the dozens of taxis are that hail us each day. A walk of 100 feet tells us why: the streets are two feet deep in water and only the bravest mopeds and cars try to bull their way through. We press on, wading through the lakes in the street amid motorbikes that plunge around us like sea horses.

"The town has been turned into a river!" Jeannette yells over the splashing.

I stoop down to put on my sandals and a passing bus swamps my pack and my guitar, which starts floating away down the street.

"All you can do is laugh, right?" Jeannette says as a van throws another roostertail our way, splashing us from head to toe. "Is your guitar okay?"

"It'll dry off, no harm done. Wood loves water, I hope."

Kuta and neighboring Denpasar are the urban heart of Bali. If you're looking for the storybook Bali of legend, along with greetings by a jewel-eyed green goddess with six beckoning arms, this ain't it. It's a tourist inferno, much like Tijuana, where Aussie frat boys come to get shit-faced drunk. The town is full of trinket and clothing stores, market stalls and open-air restaurants piled up in a landslide down a winding road to the sea. There we find a beach so filthy with litter that we wouldn't dream of lying on the sand, much less take a chance on the sewage of the sea.

There are also dozens of touts lining every street, anxious to know if we need a taxi, a tour, a t-shirt or a massage, desperate to earn a few rupees. The majority of Indonesia's 240 million people live on the neighboring island of Java, which has the second-highest population density on earth, after Bangladesh. Bali doesn't seem to be far behind.

"It's a long way from the dingo sneaking around our campsite looking for a boot to steal, isn't it?" I say, recalling the sleepless nights bathed in sweat back in the Top End.

After nearly three months of camping, I thought we might like a dab of luxury and had booked five nights at a 4-star hotel in Kuta. Mistake. I was aware that Kuta had lost its mojo with the backpacking set some 20 years ago, but wasn't prepared for its maelstrom of urban snarl.

"This is like those towns in China that you imagine are going to be quaint little villages until you get there and find out they have a population of two million people," I say as we trudge past a glut of souvenir shops in search of an ATM.

"Yes, but we've got each other, and we'll make the best of it," says Jeannette. This is her standard response whenever I get down.

"I guess the good news is that we're millionaires here," I say after leaving the ATM. "I just got us one million Indonesian rupees."

Jeannette is impressed. "Holy crapazoids! How much is that?"

"About $100, U.S."

Cat Shit Coffee

It turns out that the finest coffee in the world comes out of the arsehole of the nocturnal civet cat.

It's one of those things you learn while traveling around the quiet side of Bali.

A bit smaller than a bobcat, these critters live in the rainforest among the shade-grown coffee trees. The cats like to eat the red coffee berries and one thing leads to another and they crap them out.

Somewhere back in time, some seer collected these coffee bean turds from the jungle floor and brewed them.

Turns out that the excreted coffee beans of the civet cat are among the most flavorful and expensive in the world. It runs $25 for two ounces of cat shit coffee. Connoisseurs insist on drinking only coffee pooped out by wild civet cats, and not those held in captivity.

We stop at a coffee plantation and see a couple of these red-eyed cats in their cages.

"They look like they'd been crying," Jeannette says. "They look miserable."

"And who can blame them?" I say. "They're stuffed full of coffee beans every day and who knows what sort of laxatives."

I'm tempted to try some, but it's $5 for a demitasse cup, which is twice what you'd pay for a jumbo cuppa' joe in the U.S. It's the price of a thimble full of coffee that guides my conscience, rather than a cat's raw colon.

Travel often puts you into situations where there are moral issues relating to animal cruelty. Should you ride a tourist horse that looks abused and underfed? Pet a tiger cub on a short leash that's tormented all day by tourists? Support the torture of cattle by attending a bull-fight?

The impulse is to have the experience on the grounds that abusing animals in a bull arena or a tiger preserve is a local tradition. We've witnessed such things, but always with a lingering sense of remorse and regret.

The Banana Pancake Trail

A large, moon-faced monkey and her baby show up at the doorway of our guesthouse, wondering if it's okay to come in and poke around our stuff – maybe find a tasty banana or steal some underpants.

Shoo!

This is the town of Ubud in the center of Bali. A place where monkeys scampering on the roof serve as your alarm clock in the morning and the view outside your room is of terraced rice fields and misty volcanos. Celebs love the place; Mick Jagger and Jerry Hall reportedly got married here and honeymooned among the rice paddies.

Ubud is one of the crossroads of the so-called Banana Pancake Trail. If you're backpacking through Southeast Asia, chances are you'll pass through here sooner of later.

Back in the 1930s, the Indonesian government invited artists from all over the world to create an art colony in Ubud. The resulting P.R. boosted Bali's reputation as one of the most soulful destinations on earth, a place kissed by the Hindu gods.

Bali has been loved to death by the resulting stampede of tourists, but we find its quiet side while attempting to get lost in the network of rice paddies just out of town.

"These paths must be hundreds of years old," Jeannette says as we thread our way along narrow embankments through fields the color of spring. A line of ducks marches down the path ahead of us.

"I can't imagine any movie stars out here," I say as we wander past the place where Mick and Jerry spent their honeymoon. We see peasants huddled over the rice shoots, wearing straw hats as big as umbrellas, draped from head to toe in white cotton to protect themselves from the sun.

That night at an outdoor theater, a fire dancer wearing a straw hobby horse strapped around his waist leaps barefoot into a pile of flaming coconut shells. The flames leap three feet high, and he stomps on the sharp edges of the burning shells over and over again, yet there are no cuts or burns on his blackened feet. How does he do it?

"He uses the power of the mind," a local tells us. Indonesian magic. "He must go into a trance and prepare himself before he dances in the fire."

Perhaps it's some sort of hocus-pocus, but we feel the heat of the flames heavy on our faces from 30 feet away and I can't imagine stomping barefoot on coconut shards without cutting my feet to ribbons, much less while bathed in flames. And it's so much more satisfying to believe in Indonesian magic than to suspect a trick.

The Isle of Lombok

We make a dent in Bali's checklist of Hindu temples and waterfalls, but they're all swarming with tourists, making the island feel like one big theme park, BaliLand.

Anxious to see the other side of Indonesia, we catch an old ferry full of exhausted truckers to the island of Lombok. It's a passage of eight hours or so, rocking up and down on high seas to the east of Bali. The truckers are skinny as alley cats, sprawled asleep on the ferry's dingy seats, dressed in work clothes that don't appear to have been changed in weeks.

Lombok is the hip, new destination for backpackers searching for the laid-back side of Indonesia, highly recommended in guidebooks written for the adventure travel set. Beyond its shores lie the islands of Sumbawa, Komodo (home of the self-same dragon), Flores and East Timor. Our plans to make a stab at these places are dashed by the advent of the rainy season, which makes passage over the sea difficult or impossible.

"It's probably for the best," I say. "Every year, you read about some ferry in Indonesia or the Philippines flipping over with hundreds of people drowning."

"Now you tell me," Jeannette says, but if she's worried, it's not enough to look up from her book.

"Well, I promised you an adventure."

"Let's save that one for another time."

The local Islamic government is intent on turning Lombok into the "Island of 1,000 Mosques," while also hyping it as an international tourist destination.

Thus, you see people donating their scant cash to build opulent mosques in every town amid squalor and trash piled up in the streets. Some of the villages are indescribably filthy, with non-degradable trash strewn everywhere for lack of municipal sanitation systems. And despite the government mandate, Indonesia provides no funding for the mosques; by tradition their construction must come entirely from local contributions. It's the kind of hare-brained idea that comes from mixing government with religion.

At a boat launch, we bump into Karen, an American nurse who's been traveling solo through Asia for the past 13 months.

"What do you think of all the mosques they're building?" Jeannette asks.

"I hate it," Karen says. "The whole Muslim thing here makes for a really ugly vibe with their attitude towards women and the call to prayer five times a day. That's not going to help with tourism."

"I kind of like hearing the call to prayer," I say of the ululating cry of the muezzin heard each morning when the roosters crow. "But I once heard of a tourist who was attacked by a mob for complaining that the call was waking her up too early. She asked if they could knock it off so she could sleep in."

"Well that was dumb."

Yet aside from her loathing of Islam's tenets, Karen is sympathetic to the merchants who bargain hard with tourists.

"They see our TV shows and what we have back home and they want what we have too," she says. "You can't blame them. They have nothing at all compared to the things we take for granted."

Since avarice here mostly involves bargaining over the difference of a few nickels for a string of pearls, Jeannette and I are happy to give the Lombokians their due. Nor can we complain about the prices on the island. At the resort town of Sengiggi, we splurge on a room on the beach that runs just $15 per night.

"Hmm. Twin beds, a hose for a shower, no sink or towels. This is traveling!" Jeannette says, delighted with our squalid quarters. Like me, she has that curious affliction whereby dumpy digs are held up as being more "authentic" in terms of having a good travel experience.

As is so often the case in the tropics, there's no toilet seat on our potty and the cold water shower is the stub of a hose jutting from the wall.

"At least there don't seem to be any cockroaches," I say, glancing to the corners of the room and imagining some Indonesian three-inchers. "Or any scorpions."

Jeannette's enthusiasm goes sour later that evening. As it turns out it's Chinese New Year and we're next door to a Chinese restaurant-disco, which blasts Cantonese pop loud enough to shake the walls of our hotel into the early hours of the morning.

"All you can do is laugh, right?" I say as we endure the roar, wide awake and clasped tight together in our narrow bed.

My knowledge of Indonesia is limited to some old "Terry and the Pirates" comics from the '40s; a bit of history about the Spice Islands and the Dutch colony at Batavia; and a love of the seafaring novel, *The Wake of the Red Witch*. That's the book where a skin diver gets his foot stuck in a giant man-eating oyster shell at the bottom of the sea while going after a legendary pearl - great stuff.

"Do you know that they used to execute prisoners in Indonesia by stuffing the victim's head into a bag full of pepper?" I ask Jeannette. "They'd tie the bag around the guy's neck and then beat on it with sticks."

"What good would that do?"

"Beating the bag would produce a cloud of pepper dust and the agony of coughing to death."

"That's the kind of thing I don't want to know about," she says.

"I can think of better ways to go."

Otherwise, Jeannette and I know nothing at all about this country of 18,307 islands, which is one of the largest in the world. The Indonesians speak a babel of 583 languages and endure scores of regional governments, said to be among the most corrupt in the world. And as was the case with our visit to the Top End, we've arrived at the wrong time of year on the brink of the rainy season with virtually no foreigners on the island. Lombok is all ours.

Visiting Indonesia during the rainy season means lower prices, but also an anxious bunch of locals who are desperate to catch our attention in the hope of making a few rupees before the last of the tourists disappear.

"What do you do when the rainy season comes?" I ask Loudin, a guide who spends three days showing us around Lombok.

"Everything shuts down in February when the big rains come," he says. "We sleep. We visit family. We relax. After working so much it's good to do nothing for a few months."

High on a Volcano

Some adventure travelers like to go it alone, facing every hassle and planning every tortuous link of their trips in the spirit of Daniel Boone. But sometimes a local guide offers a wiser course. So we're glad to have Loudin, who leads us into village scenes and island hideaways that we'd never find on our own.

Loudin speaks good English. He grew up Catholic on the island of Flores and is the rare islander to break free of the cycle of poverty in the rice fields. He was selected by the priests of his school for an advanced education and thus has a high-prestige job on Lombok as a tour guide with a Land Rover and an assistant who serves as the driver.

Loudin's enthusiasm for guiding us warmed by several degrees when he saw my guitar. It turns out he plays too, and we have a great time jamming each evening with Jeannette on tambourine. Loudin shares some Indonesian folk songs, which tell of the simple life here in the islands. He also does a good cover of "Country Roads" and we wrap it up with Bob Marley's "Redemption Song." As is the case all over the developing world, everyone loves to play Bob Marley.

In the trekking town of Sennaru, Jeannette and I sit cross-legged on a small wooden platform in a garden on the side of a volcano draped in mist. A cool breeze whispers in the trees, promising more rain this evening, and in the valley below we see a grid of rice paddies bordering the sea. Up the mountain is a waterfall, cascading more than 100 feet through the rain forest.

"Volcanoes seem so much more alive than mountains," I say, gazing at a wall of trees climbing the slope across the valley. "You feel like you're riding on the back of some huge beast that could roar to life at any moment."

"Maybe it's because they *can* roar to life at any moment," Jeannette says.

The quiet side of Indonesia offers storybook visions of rain forests, volcanoes and rice paddies that few westerners ever see. We take a small outrigger across a choppy sea to an island camp, spending the night in a bamboo tree house and dining on fish grilled over an open fire. We're the only guests on the island, but during the tourist season from June through August, the camp accommodates as many as 90 foreigners, carousing around a beach bonfire. Stepping from the shore, I plunge into a garden of coral in brilliant blues and red, snorkeling in deep water just 30 feet from the beach.

The rice farmers of Lombok apparently do well compared to their neighbors on overpopulated Java; many have small but pleasant brick homes, satellite TV and motorbikes. But theirs is a life of relentless toil; first scattering the rice seed to germinate it, then planting the young shoots by hand in a muddy paddy, then laying the threshed rice along the roadside to dry. When the rice season is over, they plant tobacco or chilis.

Our vehicle wrings its way through a farm town where a market has packed the road with shoppers elbowing for room. The faces passing our window look glum to the point of hostility.

Elsewhere, we wander through a traditional village of palm-thatch lodges built on stilts to rise above the bugs, rats and heavy rains of the tropics. Pigs and chickens wander along dirt paths and there are only a few kids and old folks around. A few grandmas nod and smile as we walk timidly past. Most of the villagers are out fishing or tending their paddies.

Well-off travelers from the West often comment that people toughing it out in developing nations are poor, yet happy. Perhaps, but it's hard to imagine that living in this dull, dusty village where time has stopped for millennia could result in much pleasure. There's nothing here to enliven the senses: no electricity, books, newspapers, radio, TV or Internet. A Thoreau might argue that one is better off without such distractions, but then, he was a BS'er on such things. While living a semi-solitary life for a short time on Walden Pond, he lived a short walk down from his mother, who did his laundry and made him meals while he pontificated against modernity.

"It's like seeing how people lived for thousands of years," I say as we wander beneath the eaves of the village huts, a worried chicken clucking in our path.

"Or like how half the people on earth are still living," Jeannette says. "We wouldn't last a week."

Among the Lotus Eaters

In *The Odyssey*, Odysseus and his men land on the island of the lotus eaters and find it so enchanting that they don't ever want to leave. Quite possibly, they had stumbled onto the island of Gili Trawangan.

The Gilis are an archipelago of three small islands a few miles to the northwest of Lombok. Gili Trawangan caters to the global backpacking set, while the other two are settled by natives.

It's pandemonium as we wait on the shoreline at the end of a dirt road with a mob of Indos waiting for ferries to the Gilis. The passengers include stout women wearing head scarves and clutching babies with baskets of supplies, along with scrawny men in loose clothing donated by thrift shops from the West.

Using sign language and grunts we are directed to a long, skinny, wooden boat and wade into the surf to climb aboard. The decrepit ferry looks ridiculously tippy and incapable of handling the big swells that have paralyzed other ships at the moment. But bobbing up and down on the waves, I reflect that this boat is probably of the same design that has plied the waters of Indonesia for 1,000 years.

After the dinginess of Sengiggi Beach and the lack of westerners on Lombok, we expect much the same from Gili Trawangan. It's a surprise to find the island swarming with backpackers, lounging in bikinis and Speedos outside palapa-roofed bungalows on the beach, with restaurants, bars and shops strewn along a sand road.

"It's like we've stepped through a portal into another world," I say as we hail a passing horse cart.

There are no cars on the island, only horses and bicycles. Palapa-roofed bungalows on the beach run $25 per night, about one-tenth of what you'd pay in Hawaii. Only three miles around, Gili reminds us of other backpacking magnets: Phi-Phi Island in Thailand or Isla Grande in Brazil, with the same lanes of sand filled with exotic people from around the world.

We find a beach hut at the north end of the island and bump into a fellow American who's here for six weeks, taking a break from his gig as an independent businessman in China. Apparently, China is brimming with opportunities for young entrepreneurs from other lands.

"You don't meet many Americans here," he notes, eyeing our packs piled in a heap by the bar. I suspect he finds us as out of place as penguins in this part of Asia.

"Yes, but now there are four of us," Jeannette says, since we've invited our new pal Karen along for a drink. Karen downs her Bintang beer in a few lusty gulps and calls for another.

For once, we Americans outnumber Germans or Australians in an exotic place.

Once again, we fall in with a crowd of musical Indonesians - skinny young guys with dreadlocks, blackened by the sun, who jam every night in the beach bar. We trade songs until late in the evening with a djembe and Jeannette's tambourine thrown in for percussion.

There's some suspense in the air, however, as to whether we'll be able to get off the island. The ferries to the mainland have been out of action for several days due to heavy seas, and no one knows when they'll run again.

Gil Trawangan is served by "fast boats," which rocket across the sea to Bali, transporting the vast majority of backpackers. But these speedboats require the safety of a flat sea; the current swells would send them tumbling over the waves to a watery grave. An English traveler tells us he was stuck on the island for six weeks once because the seas were too rough to depart.

'I Promised You An Adventure'

A pocket-sized paradise gets old fast, and with the fast boats to Bali cancelled for yet another day, we decide take a chance on taking the much larger car ferry back on Lombok, about 40 miles away. Trouble is, no one on Gili Trawangan knows for sure if the car ferries are running due to the fact that the sea swells can rise 10 feet or so.

The motorboat back to Lombok is uneventful, but we have a Mad Max taxi ride through the usual maze of motorbikes and bun-tightening, head-on traffic down several backroad detours. At one point our taxi comes within a half-inch of tumbling sideways into a canal as we creep around a stalled truck on a narrow bridge. We near the port only to find that the ferry is impossible to reach due to a combination of roadwork and a mile-long traffic jam. And you know, tick, tick, tock, time is wasting.

Our driver takes it in stride, laughing and shrugging at yet another box canyon. Smiles and shrugs in the face of adversity seem to be a leading Indonesian characteristic. The Indonesians are nothing if not mellow; I imagine they must be murderous in the extreme when they blow.

After bouncing around numerous country roads past rice paddies, villages and water buffaloes with several dead-ends, we finally make the port and hike in a half mile past hundreds of trucks through the heat, dust and exhaust.

"How you holding up?" I ask Jeannette as we march into the port like conquerors. It's our little check-in phrase; something I ask her a half-dozen times a day.

"I'm doing great," she says, oiled with sweat and caked with dust under the weight of her pack. "We made it!"

"You're a cool cucumber. Anyone else would have a meltdown."

"It's just what I do," she smiles.

On the ferry, I look around for the toilet and find a room with what appears to have the sort of pee-against-the-wall urinals that are found all over Australia. But something's not quite right here, and before doing the honors, I take a moment to glance around the corner to a darkened room with several rugs on the floor. I scuttle back in alarm; it's a Muslim foot bath for use before saying one's prayers! Can't imagine the shit storm that would have kicked up if this infidel had desecrated a holy foot bath. Like, man overboard.

The ferry takes most of the day and half the night bumping the waves across the sea between Lombok and Bali. As the hours drag on with no land in sight, I begin to worry that we've gotten on the wrong boat and are headed for Sulawesi, formerly the Celebes, which is north of Java. It's supposed to be a rough place with one foot still in the Stone Age.

Our scroungy old tub rocks enough on the waves to give some of the truck drivers the heaves. "Urrkkk... bleah!" There are a few backpackers on board, but mostly it's weary truckers, sacking out in their sweaty clothes on the torn vinyl of the benches in a forward cabin.

Finally, as the sun sinks into the west, I see the shadow of a mountain far off in the mist. We'll be arriving in the port of Padang Bai long after dark.

Has there every breathed a traveler who didn't fear landing on a darkened shore? An unknown coast may harbor rocks, or pirates. Fear creeps over me as darkness falls over the sea. I feel like a scared little kitty cat, clinging to a tree, a familiar feeling from other trips. Much later, I read the words of travel veteran, Paul Theroux: "...it's in the nature of travel to be uncomfortable, if not scared silly."

I'm not scared silly, but am well aware that a traveler is always vulnerable; indeed, at the mercy of any thugs who select you as an opportunity. As a traveler, you're alone, perhaps tens of thousands of miles from home, and none of the locals might know or care if you turn up in a ditch with your throat cut and your pockets empty.

For this reason, I also feel a sense of guilt for dragging Jeannette off to iffy places. What will I say to her kids if the worst comes to pass?

I remind myself that I'm the "expedition leader" and have to buck up, wrestling a sense of hysteria with a pep talk.

"I don't know where we'll stay tonight," I say as the ferry slides towards the lights of the dock. "Handling the logistics of finding a place to stay every night really gets to me after awhile."

"Oh, we'll figure something out," Jeannette says, carefree about arriving in a darkened port at 11 p.m. "We can just stay here tonight."

"Yeah, but we don't know if there will be anyplace to stay, and then what? We'll be stuck sleeping in a doorway."

"That would be a first."

Jeannette's lack of concern exasperates me. "Aren't you ever afraid?" I ask. "I mean, for all you know, we're landing on the moon here."

"I don't freak out because I let you freak out for me," she says.

"Seriously."

"No, I don't worry because I've learned that being afraid of something doesn't help," she says. "I just have to go with the flow and be strong about it. We can't change what's going to happen, so we've just got to be smart and careful. Plus, I know you don't take any chances. I know you will find us a place.

"I can't worry," she adds after a moment. "I told the kids before we left that if anything should happen to us, they have to remember that dad and I have had a great trip and a great life together. I told them that if something happens to us, don't grieve, because we were doing what we love."

As usual, my anxiety about arriving in a strange place late at night is groundless.

Drenched in truck fumes, we arrive at the hubbub of the port and are hustled by an unexpected swarm of cab drivers. One seems trustworthy enough and we head for Kuta, 40 miles away. Trucks are lined up for 10 miles along the road outside the port due to the cancellation of several ferries over the past two weeks. It looks like the staging of an invasion.

No sooner do we get out of the port than hell's bells opens up with a monstrous deluge. Soon, we're hydroplaning through lakes in the road in a high-speed, toe-curling ride.

"As I've often said, the most dangerous part of travel is being at the mercy of a foreign driver and the oncoming traffic," I say as we crash through yet another pond in the road.

"It feels like we're on a jet ski," Jeannette says. "How do the people on motorbikes keep from getting killed out there?"

Around us, we see Indonesians flying through the rain in the dark at high speeds on their mopeds, thinly wrapped in plastic raincoats and barreling toward what looks like certain death. There's no requirement to attend driving school in Indonesia; you just apply for a license and gun it without any driver's training at all. The result: we've seen several people lying in the roadways in the aftermath of collisions.

We make it to Kuta near midnight where our driver gets hopelessly lost while the rain floods over the curbs, creating a river that's a foot deep or more. The van begins to stall as we plow through the waves and it's raining so hard we almost can't see. We're fucked!

"Just go home," we tell our anxious driver. "We'll figure it out."

And we do, splashing through town in the dark, empty streets with our soaking packs until we find a hotel. On Legian Street we see hundreds of the infamous Australian party kids, clamoring around cavernous discos that thump like cannon shells. Some of the discos are gathered around the Bali Bombing Monument, where members of the Islamic Brotherhood killed about 250 club kids with a series of bombs back in 2002.

It's easy to understand why the Islamic fanatics hate the braying, white, nightclubbing youth, who are as rich as millionaires by comparison to the average Indonesian. Even to dance hall veterans such as ourselves they come across as unbearable louts walking around shirtless in flip-flops or peekaboo miniskirts, falling down drunk and yelling obscenities down the street. But aren't we all uncouth at that age?

Thai This

"If you want to make God laugh, tell him your plans."

- Jewish proverb

The "ongoing ticket" is the curse of 9/11 and the age of terrorism. It's no longer possible to be a freewheeling traveler, rambling wherever fate blows you, because at every border crossing you run the risk of being asked to produce an ongoing ticket to prove that you won't be overstaying your welcome.

Back in Darwin, the airline staff refused to let us on the plane to Bali unless we had an ongoing ticket to leave Indonesia once our visit was over. I explained that we planned to travel by bus or train across the length of Java and then cross over to Malaysia by boat.

"Sorry, you need an ongoing ticket or we can't let you on the plane," the agent said.

In other words, extortion on behalf of the airlines.

Under the gun with only minutes to spare before the plane's departure, we asked for ongoing tickets to fly out from Yogyakarta, a big tourist destination in Indonesia. The ticket agent had never heard of the place, even though it's within spitting distance of Australia.

"He means Jakarta," said a helpful woman behind me in line.

"No, I mean Yogyakarta," I responded.

"It's Jakarta," she insisted.

"It's Yogyakarta."

Yogyakarta is the cradle of Indonesian civilization. Located in central Java, it is best known for its proximity to the largest Buddhist temple city on earth, Borobudar, one of the wonders of Asia. Yogya is also a shopping mecca which lures millions of shoppers.

But after a couple of weeks in overpopulated Bali, we incur a case of buyer's remorse over the decision to fly out of Yogyakarta, a place where human beings are packed even tighter. The misanthrope in me doesn't care to be neck-deep in more people.

"Plus, I don't care if we see another temple," Jeannette says. "I'm templed out."

I agree, thinking of all the dreary cathedrals and temples we've trudged through in our years together, filled as they are with bric-a-brac and golden doodles.

It's a no-brainer. "Let's go to Thailand instead."

With a wave of my much-abused credit card, we are on our way.

Carefree Thailand, that happy "land of smiles" where no one gives a damn if you've got an ongoing ticket. The Thais would just as soon you stayed on forever, providing you keep spending.

That night we find ourselves at a seafood feast in grungy Patong on the Thai island of Phuket. We dine at a outdoor fish market under bare lightbulbs, sitting at plastic tables and chairs, but with fresh fish, lobster, tiger prawns, squid, shark and more laid out on ice in an area that goes on for 50 yards or so.

Patong Beach is a sprawling city by the Andaman Sea that offers both the glitz and the sleaze of Las Vegas. Although it's badmouthed far and wide as the sex tourism capital of Asia, it has an undeniable energy that draws tens of thousands of visitors each year.

They certainly don't come for the scenery. We see hundreds of incredibly fat German and Russian tourists basking on the beach like whales. A couple of blubbery German gals sunbathing topless makes for an unforgettable sight because each weighs 300 pounds or more.

"That's the kind of sight you can't erase from your memory," I mutter as we walk the mile-long beach.

Patong's sex tourism can get in your face, literally. On the main street you get dunned constantly to check out the "ping-pong pussy" and "fucking show" live sex acts. But it's not all squishy-squishy, wink, wink. We spend hours seeking out presents to send back home.

"What a great place," I say as we browse the markets.

"There's so much to do," Jeannette agrees. "This is a people-watching paradise."

"You know, most backpackers think of Patong as the biggest bummer in Thailand. No one comes here because it's so gross and it's all about shopping."

"But where else can you find a purse shaped like an elephant?" Jeannette says, dangling a market treasure.

Patong is also the land of the lady boys, who dance on table tops for tourists on the main drag through town. These are young Thai men who resemble beauty queens, wandering up and down the main street in tutus and wedding gowns. One can only imagine this leads to some "Crying Game" scenarios for drunken tourists.

Legend has it that an American tourist tried to pick up a lady boy, not realizing that she was a he. His would-be conquest sat up on the bar and spread his legs to show the lucky ferangi what he was in for. The guy choked and ran.

We share a table at a fish market with two German men leering over their beauteous bar girls. Don't they notice that the girls are wearing turtle necks to hide their Adams apples?

But quite possibly, ladies hiding cocks beneath their panties are just what these guys are looking for.

The Drunk on the Bus

Drunks and buses seem to go together and such is the case as we head east across Thailand.

"Do you girls want a drink? I'm gonna' have a drink," says the red-headed drunk on the bus. He flips the tab on a warm tall boy and pours half the beer down his hairy chest.

"I'm fuckin' drunk!" he announces with a whoop.

No shit. While crossing the Thai peninsula we crowd into a busload of backpackers and find this aging Australian poking at the girls in the next seat. He's shirtless and shoeless, wearing only a pair of Thai pajama pants and a head scarf with a cloth passport pouch around his neck. His weathered, sunburned face is a quilt of angry red cuts and bruises from a fight.

"Where's my pack?" he mumbles. "Where's me fuckin' pack?"

"You left it at the hotel," says his reluctant traveling companion, a backpacker in his 20s who looks to be nursing an epic hangover. Apparently, he met the drunken Aussie at a beach party last night and is now stuck with his new buddy. The guy looks to be in his late 30s, a Peter Pan partier who never grew up.

"Well fuck it," he says in a low voice.

We gather that he's made a career of rowdy fun, relying on the kindness of strangers to mooch his way around the tropics. I begin composing a song in my head, "The Drunken Bum of Thailand," praying the guy will keep his distance. But he's falling-down-drunk and soon enough he does so, sprawled out on the floor of the bus and moaning in his sleep for the rest of the trip.

Island Hopping

When it comes to travel destinations, it's hard to beat Thailand, assuming that you visit when the Thais aren't gearing up for a revolution or a coup. Even then, nothing stops the tourist trade.

Island-hopping on the Andaman Sea and the Gulf of Thailand is a pleasure beyond words. We catch a ferry to Koh Phi Phi, gliding past hundreds of limestone karst islands which rise in towering pillars from the sea.

Koh Phi Phi is a hatchet-shaped island where 2,000 people were swept away at Christmas, 2004, when a tsunami struck one side of the island with a 15-foot wave, sweeping across a narrow isthmus to smash against a nine-foot wave coming from the other side.

Today, Phi Phi is being loved to death with a different sort of tidal wave of new hotels and shops. Its sandy lanes are packed with thousands of backpackers from around the world.

But as with sex, even when it's bad it's pretty good, and Phi Phi caters to (almost) any desire with its fire dancers on the beach and car-free walkways through the village. It's a la-la land of sun, buttery seafood, brekky on the beach, massage huts and grimacing, bloody tourists getting tribal tattoos with bamboo needles.

We move on to Koh Samui, one of Thailand's most beautiful islands, and spend five days vegging out at a small beach resort at the far end of things. On the bus ride there, we hear some excited kids talking about the upcoming Full Moon Party on nearby Koh Pha Ngan.

The full moon parties of Thailand attract up to 30,000 people, energized by a blend of Red Bull, acid, ecstasy, reefer and hard liquor. Dawn brings the bodies of moaning party people tangled in heaps amid puddles of vomit, some, perhaps, wondering where their bikini bottoms went.

"Just our sort of thing, 40 years ago," I whisper to Jeannette.

Coincidentally, we'd been planning to spend a couple of days on Pha Ngan, but thousands of young backpackers have swarmed the island, booking every cheap room.

"I don't think we'd be up for sleeping on the beach, and that's what we might get stuck with if we go," I say, talking myself out of a night of psychedelic mayhem.

"I'll go if you want to," Jeannette says, always game.

"Drop acid and dance through the night?"

"Well, I wouldn't mind dancing all night."

"I'm sure you'd dance everyone into the ground," I say.

As for LSD, I recall some good times as a teenager, driving a '65 Dodge Dart that stretched like a slinky around the curving licorice of neon freeways in old Detroit, or riding my motorcycle down the three lanes of Woodward Avenue, high on acid at the age of 19. But I also recall the bad trip at a rock festival where I vowed to drown myself in a nearby river because thousands of concert-goers had turned into slobbering, rubber-faced monsters. It made me fearful of crowds for a decade or so. LSD illuminates the sensation that all things in the universe are connected, but I'm no longer fool enough to take that trip.

And the truth is, Jeannette and I tend to hit the sack early and are up with the roosters. This seems to be a side effect of traveling through the tropics, where 5 a.m. comes up in a blaze. Our chief indulgence is a side-by-side massage on one of the hundreds of platforms lining the beach, where Thai girls work us over with coconut oil for $6 per hour. The rate is so ridiculously low that we throw in 100 percent tips.

"I'm in heaven," Jeannette murmurs over and over again as we lay on couches overlooking the surf.

A Thai massage can be intense. A 100 lb. masseuse sits on my back, digging her thumbs into my temples while her feet dig into my neck. Her thumbs are like ball-peen hammers.

We spend our nights cruising up and down Koh Samui's main drag, people-watching and looking over the same souvenirs and t-shirts. It gets old fast for me, but Jeannette enjoys herself and it dovetails with my theory that women are hard-wired to shop by dint of the hundreds of thousands of years they spent gathering firewood and foraging for food.

One of the greatest kindnesses a husband can offer his wife is to be patient about the shopping ritual; it fulfills some primal need in women.

But spending is another thing, so I, in turn, am blessed that Jeannette would rather look than buy.

1,000 Details

Traveling around the world isn't the fun-all-the-time adventure that you might imagine. There are a thousand details and connections to keep track of, resulting in a constant state of tension.

Currency, for instance. How much is 5,000 Thai baht worth? How much for 1.5 million Indonesian rupees? We will be in Malaysia for next week; how much is their money worth? What does 15,000 Singaporean dollars go for these days?

Usually these computations must be made and internalized at the airport prior to walking out into a swarm of frenzied taxi drivers. How do you know what's a fair price for a cab?

Lodgings: we will be in Kuala Lumpur in a couple of days, a city of 7 million people. How do we figure out where to stay? What about in Melaka, the Muslim town 100 kilometers down the road?

Then there are cultural considerations. When a taxi heads down a dirt road in a rough side of town, are you being abducted, or is he just taking an alley to avoid gridlock?

Must you worry about your luggage being stolen in the bus station?

What about missing your connections?

Luggage we don't worry about because our valuables are always stowed around our necks or in our daypacks, including our passports and iPad. There's nothing in our main packs that can't be replaced. As for missed connections, in Asia another taxi is always poised to appear with the wave of a hand.

There are other worries that you can't control. Is the ATM on a dodgy corner rigged to steal your account information? Does it even work? Is it picky about which cards it accepts? I have both Visa and Master Card ATM accounts and check them every few days to see if they've been compromised. Since Asia tends to be the "land of cash only," we rarely use credit cards, but still, they must be checked periodically to see if they've been hacked.

Then there are a host of mundane concerns: booking rooms and airfares down the line, sunburn, the threat of food poisoning, hazardous walkways, language difficulties, oncoming traffic, reckless taxi drivers, the undertow, problems back home, bugs, noisy discos near your hotel, lack of exercise, long lines in airports...

It all adds up, and there are times when a locker room pep talk is needed with the reminder that we're on an expedition of sorts and not a vacation, so toughen up. On a vacation, most of your logistical problems are resolved before you even leave home. But on a trip around the world, the stress comes with the experience of winging it from one unknown place to another.

Riding the Dragon

At 4 in the morning, the outskirts of Bangkok look as though they've suffered a neutron bomb attack. In the darkness before dawn are miles of featureless, steel-shuttered buildings, shrouded in cobwebs of electrical wires without a soul around.

We've arrived here after a 15-hour trip by ferry and bus up the long peninsula of southern Thailand from Koh Samui. The buses in this side of the world are marvels beyond anything we know in America - towering double-deckers with luxurious reclining seats, velour blankets, onboard video, snack and beverage service, albeit with freezing air-conditioning. Fantastic airbrush paintings of everything from mythical Thai scenes of gods and serpents to cartoon characters decorate the sides of every bus.

Jeannette was out cold last night by 8:30, but since we were roused (repeatedly) for full dinners, courtesy of the VIP government bus service, we got it together to watch a new Justin Timberlake film on our iPad with the full moon coming through the window.

The road gets rougher as we near Bangkok, and the huge bus sways and bobs over the potholes. We snuggle under our saris against the chill of the air conditioning.

"It feels like we were riding on the back of a dragon," I mumble in Jeannette's ear in the darkness before dawn.

"Just the two of us, far out in the world, riding on a dragon. I love you," she breathes, half asleep.

"I love you too." Sleep, bounce, sleep, bounce as the dragon lumbers on.

We arrive at the backpacker haven of Khao San Road just ahead of Bangkok's notorious rush hour. Thousands of backpackers from around the world pack the hotels and bars of the Banglamphu neighborhood in and around Khao San Road. It's a 24-hour carnival of vendors, food carts and cafes serving up heaping platters of seafood awash in Beer Chang, all spilling into the street. It's the Bourbon Street of Asia, only without the music.

Although it's 5 in the morning, the bars along Khao San are overflowing with backpackers who've been up drinking all night.

"You've got to marvel at the livers of the backpacker tribe," I say as we walk down the middle of the street to a guesthouse.

"It makes you wonder how they can afford to start drinking in the early afternoon and carry on all night until dawn," Jeannette says.

Lining the street, which is piled high with the trash of last night's partying, are a gaggle of lady boys and possibly even a few honest-to-gosh female hookers looking for one last date at dawn.

Minutes later we are lying in a four-poster bed draped in mosquito netting in an antique room done up in shades of cream and teak. A payment of 150 baht ($5 U.S.) has gotten us our room eight hours before check-in.

Bliss!

The Legend of Jim Thompson

Today, what was once the "Village of Plums" is one of Asia's largest cities with more than 9 million people living in and around Bangkok. Some of Bangkok's success is due to the efforts of Jim Thompson, who single-handedly revived Thailand's silk industry.

Thompson was an American businessman who was recruited by the OSS (Office of Strategic Services) in World War II, the forerunner of the CIA. He was on his way to Thailand in 1945 when the Japanese surrendered. After his military service ended, he decided to stick around and got involved in Thailand's declining silk industry. His marketing skills were just what the poor silkworm ranchers of Thailand needed.

As it happened, Thompson knew Margaret Landon, author of *Anna and the King*, a novel about the true-life exploits of an American widow who became a governess in the Court of Siam in the 1860s. When the film, "The King and I" was released in 1951, the costumes of the musical were lush with Thai silks. Overnight, silk became the rage of the fashion world, launching Thompson's fortunes into the stratosphere, along with those of thousands of Thai silk producers.

A former architect, Thompson built an open-air mansion entirely of teak on a quiet canal in Bangkok, cobbling together several traditional homes trucked in from the countryside. The House on the Klong was filled with artwork from throughout Asia, as well as royalty, movie stars and diplomats from around the world, who rubbed elbows with Thompson's friends among the locals.

But Thompson disappeared on a trip to the Cameron Highlands in Malaysia in 1967 while visiting friends. He went out for a stroll in the forest after lunch on Easter Sunday and never returned.

A massive search was launched that went on for months, the biggest manhunt in the history of Malaysia; but the mystery of Jim Thompson continues to this day. Some believe he was hit by a truck while walking along a roadway and his body was disposed of. Another theory is that he was eaten by a tiger. Possibly, he was executed by Malaysian communists who suspected that he was a CIA spy.

Whatever the case, Thompson's legacy lives on in the success of Asia's silk industry. That, along with his home, which is now a museum destination, tucked into a quiet neighborhood surrounded by a mammoth shopping complex in the heart of Bangkok.

One night, I get the bright idea to take a ferry down the length of the Chao Phraya River to save 100 bucks on a sundown cruise.

We end up at a flea market of the sort that sells cheap tennis shoes and polyester clothing that's miles down the river, only to find that the return ferries have ended their service for the night.

Even the taxis have disappeared, so Jeannette and I begin the long walk across town through Bangkok's empty streets, which run out of sight in a canyon of darkened buildings.

Bangkok has some lively scenes after dark, including its Night Market, the Red Light district and Khao San Road, but most of the city rolls up its sidewalks as soon as the sun goes down, and that's just where we find ourselves.

An empty city after dark is an eerie place, and I feel that we are vulnerable to predators as we march through the gloom, be they thugs or cops.

"It's never good to be alone in a city without the comfort of a crowd," I say as we swing along.

"Amen to that," Jeannette answers, picking up the pace. We are almost running.

After hiking nearly an hour we reach an intersection maintaining a trickle of traffic and hail a lone tuk-tuk driver on his way home for the evening. Home, Jeeves!

We're not eager to linger in Bangkok, having been there, done that before. It's one of three supercities we're hitting over the next couple of weeks, and one can only take so much urban grit. Early the next morning we head south again, this time for Malaysia.

Malaysia

The guy sitting next to us on the monorail could pass for Osama bin Laden's kid brother at a Halloween party, having the same dreamy eyes, chest-length beard, white linen robes and headdress of a Sunni Arab. He looks like a mellow dude, however; just another traveler like us, passing through Kuala Lumpur.

Also known as KL, this city of seven million people is the capital of Malaysia. Blessed with an abundance of beaches, rain forests, hill country, volcanoes and lively cities, you'd think that Malaysia would be a vagabond's dream come true. But there are far fewer backpackers here, not like the tens of thousands up in Thailand. Perhaps this is because Malaysia is an Islamic country, which is a major buzz-kill.

After 9/11 in 2001, in the spirit of choosing up sides, the government here got the bright idea of declaring that Malaysia was officially an Islamic country. This vaporized Western tourism overnight, but had the effect of making Malaysia one of the top vacation spots in the world for Arabs from the Mideast.

Thus, you see a fair number of "letter box" ladies here from Saudi Arabia and the Emirates at the fancy shopping malls – women clad head-to-toe in black silk gowns with only a slit for their eyes. Typically, her Muslim husband is trooping alongside with no similar rules of constraint, dressed in a baseball cap, sneakers, cargo shorts and a "Party Naked" t-shirt or something out of a JC Penney's catalog. It makes for an odd couple.

Yet Malaysia also accommodates communities of Chinese, Indians, Hindus, Buddhists, Taoists and Christians. And since English is the second language here, we can read the signs on virtually every store, restaurant, product and street, making it easy to get by. Europeans have been on the scene as traders in Malaysia for 500 years, so a couple of farangs from northern Michigan are just part of the passing parade.

Over four days, we get lost and found, tramping the grimy streets of Chinatown and visiting the neck-craning Petronas Towers, recently deposed of their status as the tallest buildings on earth. We spend an afternoon gawking at Batu Cave, a hollowed-out mountain which houses a Hindu temple of giant, plaster gods. A 100-foot, golden statue of Krishna is impressive, but even more memorable is the fact that the temple is awash with garbage from hordes of Indian tourists who've gathered here for a festival. A river of trash runs down hundreds of steps from the cave, offering a glimpse of India yet to come.

Hotels run as little as $15 per night here for a backpacker squat, but rest assured, it's not all black pepper gravy and Tiger beers 'round the pool in old KL. Asian cities tend to be hot, noisy, crowded and dirty. The sidewalks are dusty, crumbling ruins and frequently blocked with motorbikes or stalls, forcing you to walk in the street amid heavy traffic, bathed in the exhaust of passing buses. Every few yards we breathe the acrid, urine-rich stink of a sewer vent, and after jostling with crowds all day in the 90-degree heat, it feels like we've been dipped in 30-weight motor oil.

But this produces the kind of anarchy that makes it possible to have a hilarious dinner of prawns and spring rolls beneath an umbrella in a thunder storm. We dine at a cafe that spills halfway into the middle of a crowded street, our feet dangling in a stream.

On the flip side, Asian cities also have chic downtown streets and cavernous shopping malls, packed with every possible Western out-let: Versace, Chanel, Dior, Papa John's Pizza, Burger King, KFC, you name it. On our first night of wandering around the streets of KL we are absolutely astounded to find a Roasters chicken franchise owned by country pop star Kenny Rogers. Who knew that the man who sang "The Gambler" and "Don't Take Your Love to Town" also served up such exquisite black pepper gravy?

Malaysia is a friendly place; its people reach out to you with sincere smiles and the spirit of acceptance. But it has its dark side. While walking down a main street we see reminders that *"Death! is the man-datory penalty for drug dealers"* on posters along the way. This is bad news for a young Nigerian soccer player who was busted at the airport yesterday with 75 packets of methamphetamine in his bowels. Necktie party for that one.

Ditto for a 23-year-old newspaper columnist from Saudi Arabia who made the mistake of conducting a fictional conversation with the Prophet Muhammad over Twitter in which he pointed out the hypocritical aspects of Islam (and there are many). In response, tens of thousands of furious Muslims demanded his execution on Facebook. He was apprehended at the KL airport, denied legal counsel, and a private jet was sent from Saudi Arabia to fetch him home for trial. We later learned that he spent 20 months in prison for imagining the human side of Muhammad.

It makes you appreciate the freedom from religion we enjoy back in the USA.

If you want to know what happened to the wealth of America, you'll find much of it in Malaysia, which is bursting with prosperity. There are new monorails, subways, roads, freeways, shopping malls and housing projects everywhere. Not to mention thousands of factories that fled America, taking U.S. jobs along with them.

"You'd think we were in the suburbs of southern California, rather than a country that was stuck in the third world a generation ago," I say as our bus rolls through the suburbs south of KL. We glide along a new freeway with impeccable landscaping past miles of new apartment towers and housing developments.

"Makes you want to buy a condo here, doesn't it?" Jeannette says.

"Oh sure, but there goes the neighborhood with us not being Muslims. By the way, did you know this is our 100th day of traveling together? We've been together almost every minute of the whole trip."

"I know, and I haven't missed home at all. I'd like to just go on traveling forever."

"You're a free bird, baby."

"That's how I fly," Jeannette says, making a bird call that turns the heads of passengers in front of us.

"Think of how many people would freak out if they had to spend every minute for months on end with their spouse," I say.

"Yeah, but they're not us. We know how to give and take."

"Whenever I've traveled alone the hardest part was not having anyone to share things with," I say, reflecting on my solo trip around the world. "You might see a fantastic sunset or climb a mountain, but if there's no one there to share the moment, it gets lonely. Time drags on forever because you have 16 hours to fill each day with only your own thoughts for company."

"Time's not dragging for me at all," Jeannette says. "In fact, it's flying by."

"Yeah, well try traveling on your own sometime. It's different."

"I'm more worried that our trip will seem over as soon as it's started."

Lair of the Bogeyman

A wedge-headed lizard the size of an alligator swims past us as we enjoy our morning coffee by the riverside. He must be five feet long, king of the canal.

It's Valentine's Day and we're staying at a guesthouse on the river in Melaka's Chinatown, the narrow streets of which are lit by red paper lanterns at night. Outside our window we see boats gliding up and down the river and hear the eerie call to prayers of the muezzin, echoing from loudspeakers around the city.

Melaka (or Melacca) is a World Heritage town and one of Malaysia's top tourist attractions.

Four hundred years ago, Melaka was one of the most important ports in the world, considered the Asian twin of Amsterdam. Through the years it was held by Malay sultans, the Portuguese, Dutch, British, and now by tourists.

For hundreds of years, ships traveling between India and China had to pass through the 550-mile Malacca Strait between Malaysia and the immense island of Sumatra. This was necessary to catch the seasonal trade winds going to and from Asia, and to avoid the typhoons west of Sumatra. There was no other practical way for square-rigged ships to sail east or west.

So this strait was of great strategic importance, fought over for centuries. The Strait was also the haunt of the Bugai pirates, who swarmed convoys of trade ships in fleets of Chinese junks. Imagine 1,000 pirates bearing down on you with certain death just a puff of the wind away. It's from the Bugai that we got the term, "bogeyman."

'Don't Electrocute Yourself'

We leapfrog the border to Singapore on a bus, hauling our packs 100 yards from Malaysia through customs in a rush as the bus driver waves, hurry, hurry, hurry! Soon, we are deposited on a nondescript corner of the city-state without a map and spend an hour or so flailing about to get our bearings. No one speaks English and no maps of the city are to be had in the local shops. The 90-degree sun adds even more weight to our packs as we wander back and forth across streets roaring with traffic, desperate to find a reference point.

But at last we locate our bare bones hostel near Little India that caters to Asian backpackers, who are apparently not a picky bunch. Ours is an airless, windowless room about 8' by 8' for the ripoff rate of $70 per night.

I protest the rate to the dragon lady who runs the place, but she bristles that there's a big concert in town and every hostel room and cheap dive in Singapore has been scooped up by hordes of teenagers. So like it or lump it.

There's no decoration of any kind in our cell, except for a "no smoking, no eating, no drinking" sign, along with a cartoon explaining the rules: "Don't electrocute yourself." "Avoid bed bugs! No bags/luggage on the bed."

But you don't come to Singapore to sit in your room with the bed bugs, and the sights of one of the wealthiest cities in the world are ideal for two walking addicts like ourselves. We walk until we're sick with exhaustion through Little India, Chinatown and along the waterfront.

The Marina Bay Sands looms like a hallucination as we round a corner on Singapore's waterfront. It looks like an ocean liner parked atop three 55-story towers.

"Wow, where did that come from?" I wonder. Towering 600 feet over the harbor, this $5.7 billion hotel casino wasn't here when I visited just four years ago. It turns out this is the most expensive standalone casino in the world, with a luxury mall at its roots and a skypark up top that includes a garden filled with trees, gourmet restaurants and a vast infinity pool. Our bleak lodgings in Little India are light years down the scale.

"Singapore has a bad rap as being a boring city," I say as we watch a laser light show over the harbor that night.

"I don't find it boring at all," Jeannette says.

"I think some travel writer slammed the place a long time ago and others keep repeating it."

"Crapazoids, I only wish we could stay longer."

"They have a lot of fines here for spitting on the sidewalk or chewing gum," I recall. "I remember seeing a sign here that warned against peeing on elevators. It's supposed to be a big police state."

"I haven't seen a cop yet."

It's true, over two days we walk more than 20 miles around the city and don't see a single uniformed police officer. Yet the citizens of Singapore never seem to get out of line, even waiting minutes for the "Walk" sign at stoplights when there's no oncoming traffic in sight.

"Maybe they're all in plain clothes, watching our every move."

Down on the harbor we pass a jewel box of a hotel that seems right out of Georgian England. The Raffles Hotel is the legacy of Sir Stamford Raffles, who established the British port of Singapore in 1819.

Raffles was one of those comets who blaze the brightest in their youth, achieving titanic feats before burning out far too young.

Born on a ship off the coast of Jamaica in 1781 to a British captain and his wife, Stamford began working as a clerk for the East India Company at the age of 14 as a consequence of his parents being down on their luck. In 1805 he was dispatched to the faraway British outpost of Penang, an island off the coast of Malaysia, where he learned the Malay language and made himself useful to the authorities. This led to his involvement in a war against the Dutch and their French allies on the island of Java, where he served as lieutenant governor.

Following a crushing defeat of the Javanese forces, Stamford ran into a spot of trouble with accusations of bungling the island's finances and was called back to London to clear his name. There, he wrote and published *The History of Java*.

Sent east again to shape up a ruined outpost, Stamford's star rose in esteem and he was ordered to negotiate with the sultans of Malaysia for a new port to rule the Straits. He selected the isle of Singapura and directed the layout of the city.

Although Stamford introduced reforms such as ending cock-fighting and restricting slavery, he kept a large contingent of slaves at his own homes before establishing a system of importing convicts for labor.

It wasn't all feats of derring-do and diplomacy for young Stamford, however; he was devastated by the death of his wife, Olivia, who like many Europeans fell prey to the diseases of Java at an early age. He himself fell ill years later and returned to England to recover. There he established the London Zoo, becoming the first president of the

Zoological Society of London.

All this, and so much more by the age of 44.

With a necklace of ports that included Hong Kong, Singapore, Melaka, and Georgetown in Malaysia, the Brits did a fine job of tying up this corner of the world in the 1800s, losing it all to a tidal wave of Japanese troops in a matter of weeks in December, 1941.

Today, it's the financiers and bankers of Singapore who are calling the shots in the dependent economies of the old empires around the world. It's another case of the minnow swallowing the whale.

With cheap airfares to and from the the rest of the world, Singapore makes for an excellent travel hub for exploring Southeast Asia, but we're anxious to move on. At the airport we find ourselves in the company of dozens of grubby businessmen, hauling carts of shrink-wrapped TVs, computers, toys and other treasures home to Sri Lanka. Aside from a lone woman covered from head-to-toe in traditional dress, Jeannette is the only woman on the plane.

The Isle of Serendipity

Sri Lanka at last, an island like Tasmania that Jeannette and I never expected to see in this lifetime. Once known as Ceylon, this country was also called Serendib centuries ago. Thus was coined the word "serendipity," meaning a sweet coincidence of fate.

But serendipity seems to have come and gone in the "charming fishing village" (guidebook description) of Negombo where tourists roost after flying into the sticky capital of Colombo. Jeannette and I catch a cab from the airport with the radio tuned to a country music station playing hits by the likes of Dolly Parton (!) and walk around town amid the hubbub, hullaballoo and hurly-burly of traffic, wandering for half a mile or so through a crowded market and getting lost in this dirty old town by the sea.

Fifty years ago, the streets of Negombo were filled with elephants and donkeys instead of cars and motorbikes. The streets were laid out long before the advent of the automobile and no provision was made for sidewalks when motor vehicles claimed the right-of-way. As is the case in so many Asian cities, we have to walk amid the traffic, hoping that some incompetent driver doesn't run us over.

Sri Lanka dangles off the southern tip of India like an earring. It's an island about the size of West Virginia populated by the gentle Tamil people, who are considered a blissful bunch when they're not busy murdering each other with bombs and machine guns.

"I call it India lite," I tell Jeannette. "It will be a good way to ease into India itself, which is pretty intense."

"How long will we be in Shri Lanka?" she asks.

"It's Sri Lanka, no 'h' sound."

"Shri Lanka."

"It's 'Sri' Lanka..."

"Shri..."

"No 'h'..."

"I'm not saying an h, you're just hearing an h."

Tourism here has lurched from one disaster after another. The island was devastated by the 2004 tsunami that killed over 230,000 people across the Indian Ocean (some estimates are as high as 800,000). This was on top of its 26-year civil war with the Tamil Tigers which ended in 2009, leaving up to 100,000 dead. Thousands of Tamils are said to be languishing in tent city concentration camps in the zone of the vanquished. So the Lankans have been working on their tourism infrastructure for only the past three years by the time we arrive and still have a long way to go, renovating dilapidated hotels, some of which haven't been occupied in decades.

It's said to be a difficult place to get around, what with things being on the mend, so we hook up with an Intrepid Travel group of 12 backpackers. I welcome taking a break from the logistics of figuring out our moves each day. And back in the planning stage of our trip, it occurred to me that Jeannette might like some other company on our way around the world as a respite from 24/7 of yours truly.

Based in Melbourne and catering to backpackers, Intrepid Travel (intrepidtravel.com) offers small group tours in over 100 countries. It's one of several adventure travel companies, including G Adventures and Mountain Travel Sobek, that smooth the way if you're interested in going to difficult places or simply desire some travel companions.

China, for instance, can be tricky if you don't speak Mandarin or the Han dialect. How do you order train tickets or dinner? Jeannette and I had some luck in Shenzhen by simply pointing at what we wanted, but that sucks as a travel strategy.

So we've taken more than half a dozen trips with Intrepid Travel, including a second go at mainland China.

Established in 1988 by two Australian backpackers, today the company offers more than 800 itineraries on every continent, guiding more than 100,000 travelers each year.

Typically, a native guide leads a group of up to 12 backpackers on a route that includes home stays, exotic lodgings and excursions. The travel style ranges from rough-around-the-edges to lux options for old folks and softies. Roughly half the groups tend to be single with travelers ranging from their 20s to their 60s.

Our group makes for an assortment on par with what Chaucer imagined in *The Canterbury Tales*.

Dave and Roz are a gentle couple in their 70s, full of derring-do and committed to traveling to offbeat places. Dave was stationed in Sri Lanka in 1960 with the Royal Air Force at a time when working elephants created traffic jams on the roads.

Andy and Mandy are mountain climbers from Britain in their early 50s. They met at a Mount Everest base camp in Nepal.

Ashley, the youngest among us in her 20s, is a submachine gun-toting deckhand on an Australian customs boat that interdicts refugees from Iran, Pakistan, Indonesia and elsewhere who are trying to sneak into the Oz as illegal immigrants.

Alison is a social worker with an aid program in Washington D.C., which assists inner city residents in Detroit, Cleveland and other sink-holes of despair.

Tammy, a dental tech from Australia, is fulfilling a quest: back in the '80s, the pop group Duran Duran made a video in Sri Lanka and she's wanted to see the place ever since.

All of us are hopeless travel addicts. Why else would we be in Sri Lanka?

Heading north from Negombo on a circuit of the island, we pass a dreamlike scene of 100 outrigger fishing boats floating out to sea with tea-colored sails, just as they did 1,000 years ago. Emerald jungles flow into swamps of lotus flowers, egrets and water buffalo, and on into rice paddies and weathered palm shacks.

"I love Shri Lanka," Jeannette says as our bus speeds along. "It's so pretty."

"It's Sri Lanka."

"That's what I said!"

In the War Zone

Only a few years ago, guerilla fighters used to cross the lake next to our hotel in northeastern Sri Lanka to plant bombs and take potshots at the soldiers here. Helicopter gunships heading into battle and car bombs in the marketplace were daily occurrences, and there are still refugee camps just north of where we're staying that are filled with victims of the war.

But now that the war has ended, the Lankans are busy turning old temples and bell-shaped stupas into tourist gold, painting old hotels and sprucing up long-closed restaurants.

Tourism is the sunrise on this country's horizon. A teacher makes just $150-$200 per month here, a doctor starts at $200. One of our guides says he makes 10,000 rupees a month at his regular job as a sales clerk; his wife makes 4,000 rupees working in a pharmacy. This totals about $110 U.S. per month, and they must spend 2,500 rupees per month on their child's education. I get the impression they're doing better than most here, earning the equivalent of $1,320 per year.

Since everyone is poor, tipping is extremely important. You give a small tip to the man who guards your sandals outside the temple, a tip for the baggage boy, a tip for the bathroom attendant, and so on. Even if you've hauled your pack half a mile in the hot sun, it would be cruel not to give the hotel bellboy a tip to carry it the last 20 feet to your room. Not to mention he's desperate for something to do.

There aren't many young travelers in Sri Lanka. It's not a "cool" destination on the Banana Pancake Trail like trendy Cambodia or Laos, and certainly no party scene like Thailand. Travelers here tend to be older, experienced travel junkies who have the stamina to handle endless hikes around old temples, ancient cities and monasteries, enduring lectures on Sri Lankan history and the life of Buddha.

"I had wanted a carving of Buddha to take home, but after seeing the old guy's statue about 1,000 times now, I could care less," I say.

"More temples, temples, temples...." Jeannette says. "You look good in a skirt though."

"Thanks, it's my new look." As is the case when visiting Hindu or Buddhist temples across Asia, I'm required to wrap a sari over my shorts to avoid the sacrilege of showing my unholy knees.

Instead of pyramids, the Buddhist kings of old Serendib built bell-shaped stupas, which are like half a giant egg with a golden spire on top. We visit a whitewashed stupa that's 300 feet tall and is said to contain 100 million bricks, enough to build a road to the moon and back. Inside is buried a priceless treasure: Buddha's collar bone.

More interesting is the mountain palace of Sigiriya, a fortress and pleasure house located 600 feet high atop a butte called the Lion Rock near the center of the island.

Legend has it that young Prince Kashyapa seized the throne of a Sri Lankan kingdom back in 477 A.D. and then went on the run, fearing reprisals from competing heirs. Over an 18-year period his thousands of slaves built a palace atop an impregnable butte, filling it with his 500 concubines. The prince had his own private swimming pool and gardens here, perched high above the plains, and judging by the paintings of nubile young maidens we find in the caves on the way up, he preferred women who could fill a C cup.

"He was the Hugh Hefner of Sri Lanka," our guide Bruno says.

It wasn't always Buddhists and princes here, however. The cannibals who lived on Sri Lanka before the arrival of Buddhism 2,300 years ago worshipped a cobra god of fertility. The traditional cure for a cobra bite is to drink the urine of a child. But you'd better hope the nearest kid has to pee right away, because you simply must drink that precious urine before the venom reaches your heart. Or so the story goes.

What we get out of these ruined cities, lost empires and ghosts of long ago is that life is short and you'd better squeeze all the juice out of it while you can. Because as the song goes, we'll soon be dust in the wind, just like the long-dead kings of old Sri Lanka.

Traveling Lite

"Funny, but I'm packing less clothing on this trip than I would for a weekend in Chicago," Jeannette says, appraising her scant apparel, spread out on a hotel bed. "You'd think it would be hard living out of a backpack for seven months with hardly any clothes, but the less stuff we have to lug around, the better."

Getting rid of stuff we've bought along the way has become a never-ending quest. We're constantly on the lookout for post offices in order to mail everything from gifts to gear back home. Statues of Shiva and Ganesh go in the mail along with mirrored bedspreads, goofy ethnic hats and camping gear.

Jeannette is packing three skirts and up to six tops, while I have some nylon pants, a pair of shorts and four shirts.

Toiletries, sandals and jackets make up our essentials, but the balance of our gear is "just-in-case" stuff we seldom, if ever, use: flashlights, ponchos, bungee cords, bike lock, first aid kit, headphones, chargers, power converters, etc. It all fits into our two packs with room to spare, with neither pack weighing more than 30 pounds.

Yet it always seems like far too much stuff.

"It makes you realize that you really don't need many possessions to be happy," Jeannette says.

"Especially when you consider that a lot of Americans feel like they're poor if their family only has one car or they can't afford designer jeans," I say.

As we've learned from the people we've encountered all over the world, all you really need is to be warm, dry and well-fed. That, and a change of clean underwear.

The Not So Ugly Americans

Our bus gets a flat in a small town in southern Sri Lanka, giving us a chance to watch a protest march passing by while the tire gets fixed.

To our surprise, the marchers are protesting America.

But there's something a bit off about the protesters. About 200 well-dressed women lead the march, as gorgeous as a flower garden in their saris of sky blue, spring green, rose red and purple royale, festooned with gold and silver ribbons. Behind them march a small group of well-groomed young men wearing ties, dress shirts and pants. It looks more like a wedding than a protest march.

It turns out that these villagers have been hired by the government to stage a phony protest and photo-op against the U.S., which has threatened to condemn Sri Lanka's record on human rights at an assembly of the United Nations.

When Sri Lanka's civil war was winding down in 2009, government troops corralled tens of thousands of civilians and members of the Tamil Tigers into an area of a few hundred acres and shelled them with relentless artillery. This was followed by deforming tortures, brandings, rapes and executions. It's estimated that up to 40,000 civilians died. Online, there is evidence that the torture and rape of suspected Tiger sympathizers is ongoing.

The Sri Lankan government doesn't appreciate the U.S. condemning the atrocities or calling for an investigation, and thus has staged this demonstration, albeit at the back end of nowhere.

But this is the first hint of anti-Americanism we've seen on our trip, which hasn't been the case on other travels.

Perhaps America doesn't seem as important to the citizens of the world anymore, now that boom economies are creating huge amounts of wealth in countries such as China, Brazil, India and Russia. It's a topsy-turvy world now: Asia seems to have plenty of Russian and Chinese tourists who were impoverished prisoners in their own countries just a generation ago.

By contrast, we run into few Americans. At a hotel in the city of Kandy, I check the guest register and find page after page of visitors from France, Switzerland, Holland, Germany, Japan, Russia, Sweden... Six pages back I find the signature of a lone American traveler from Colorado.

I Want Kandy

In Kandy, we have the honor of briefly glimpsing one of Buddha's teeth.

When Buddha died 2,500 years ago at the age of 80, his body was cremated on a pyre of sandalwood. But some of his body parts were kept as relics to be spread to monasteries around Asia, including a traveling tooth.

A huge tussle was made over the tooth for centuries. Wars were fought over its ownership and elaborate temples were constructed to house it. Eventually, it found its way from India to Sri Lanka and the city of Kandy. A garden city of 1.7 million people at an elevation of 1,500 feet above sea level, Kandy offers the first cool weather we've had in four months.

We visit an ornate temple by the lake, passing under a canopy of trees where hundreds of birds shower unsuspecting visitors with torrents of shit. At the temple, hundreds of tooth-peepers are squeezed like toothpaste past a glimpse of the golden casket which houses the sacred molar. It's not the thrill you might imagine; we barely get a glimpse of it, peering at its crystal reliquary from 20 feet away over the shoulders of the crowd. Yet during the course of the day, thousands of pilgrims pay their respects to the tooth, and that's every day all year round.

Trouble stills follows the tooth around. A few years ago the Tamil Tigers bombed the temple and now you must have your bags checked to get in, with armed guards stationed at the entrance.

We find an even greater treasure in Kandy, a Pizza Hut at the End of the World.

Pizza seems almost priceless because there's never any surprise as to what you'll dine on in Sri Lanka: it's rice curry every day, meaning a selection of curried potatoes, beets, green beans, eggplant, lentils (dahl), chickpea bread and rice. Same-same every day, with some bits of chicken at dinner.

For proper dining, one must eat off a banana leaf plate with the fingers of one's right hand (the left hand is used for wiping in the toilet), rolling the food into gooey balls of rice, curry and veggies. It's the kind of dining experience a three-year-old would love.

The Wild Elephant Problem

A battered old city bus decorated with house paint provides our flying carpet as we travel down the east side of the island. Sinhalese music blasts from the loudspeakers at the front of the bus, which is garlanded with roses. The bus is jam-full and protected from crashes by a picture of Buddha gazing down on us from the front window as we weave in and out of oncoming traffic at high speeds along a narrow road.

Sri Lanka is rough around the edges, but with far fewer people than neighboring India. The streets are jammed with hundreds of three-wheel tuk-tuks, which will take you just about anywhere for a few rupees. A dozen cows wander through a dusty bus station in town past second-hand beater buses shipped here from the West. A snake charmer lures a puzzled cobra from its basket with his flute. Monks wander by in orange and burgundy robes and twisted beggars lie with hands outstretched on the temple steps. We see monkeys everywhere, picking through trash or loping along the roadside.

"The wild elephant problem" as it is called, is still a concern in this part of the world where elephants are known to trample rice paddies, gardens, homes and people. In the local news is the story of an elephant who attacked a truck at at a place where one of her loved-ones had been killed by a vehicle and was buried alongside the road. The grieving elephant makes repeated visits to the grave, lunging at passing vehicles.

Elsewhere, villagers demand that forest rangers do something about an elephant that killed a 53-year-old father of five.

"Can you imagine getting trampled by an elephant?" Jeannette wonders.

"No, I cannot," I say, although actually, I can imagine it quite well.

Trekking in the Tea

My wallet is thick with 2,000 rupee notes, worth about $18 each, and I feel the guilt of the rich when I pay a bill because the locals are forever craning their necks to see what kind of cash the Westerner is packing.

"I'm going to hide a moth in my empty wallet when we reach India so they'll think we're broke," I say.

"Just think of all the good we're doing the local economy," Jeannette says.

"We've done our bit."

Indeed, Kandy is considered a shopping paradise due to its markets stuffed with name-brand clothing, including Columbia, which is made locally. We're squired from stall to stall by scouts anxious to earn a finder's fee.

An old train takes us deep into the mountains for two days of trekking among miles of tea plantations. We hike through smoky, green-ter-raced mountains, veiled in the mist and ribboned with winding paths of crushed rock and clay. The country reminds us of the terraced farm-lands of the Urubamba River Valley in Peru, with the same lush moun-tain vistas and squalid homes of the villagers.

The tea fields go on forever, punctuated by the wretched villages of the tea pluckers, many of whom sustain their hard lives by staying drunk day and night on a cheap liquor called arak. Even the kids drink this poison, and some of them look it, with pinched faces that are gaunt with malnutrition and the haggard look of substance abuse.

The tea pickers are all women who work from dawn to dusk for what would be considered spare change in America. By one account, Sri Lanka's 150,000 tea pickers make about $4 per day, which must be surrendered to local stores as part of an eternal chain of debt. "But if the overseer feels they've done a bad job of picking a row of tea bushes, they receive nothing for the day," our guide Bruno says.

Most of the tea pluckers live in mosquito-infested, tumble-down huts with rusting sheet metal roofs that wouldn't pass for chicken coops in America.

We have a lively time playing music for some kids at a day care in their village, however; me on guitar and Jeannette on tambourine. Huge smiles from the kids.

"I guess I haven't gotten the day care business out of my system yet!" Jeannette says, beaming with joy at being surrounded by two dozen excited children.

Evening brings a night in what was once a plantation manager's home. It's a decrepit estate in genteel decline which harkens back to the days when the sun never set on the British Empire. With teak trim and dusty antiques from a century ago, these hill country estates take you back to the time of the Kipling, hot toddies, starched collars and tea time in the afternoon.

The British Raj built Sri Lanka's railways and bridges and tarred the roads, but much has fallen into ruin since they left. The Sinhalese traded the evils of colonialism for the nepotism and corruption of self rule.

Weird scenes: A large black scorpion chases a terrified mouse across the hotel porch; a frog makes itself at home in our shower; a fellow traveler finds a centipede in his bed; another is suffering from an ulcerating spider bite, requiring a heavy dose of antibiotics. And does anyone need the vial of sea salt I've brought along to deal with leeches? Jeannette needs a sprinkle after our trek through the jungle and the tea fields.

Heaven & Hell

Sri Lanka has an antidote to its temple treks: a necklace of beaches ringing the southern half of the island. We spend two days at the seaside resort of Mirissa, heaven by the sea after bouncing around on buses for a couple of weeks. Our respite includes prawn dinners by firelight, body surfing, and no hassles from local hawkers, who are kept out of bounds. The southern beaches are a magnet for travelers from around the world.

Mirissa was wiped out by the tsunami of 2004, which killed 49,000 Sri Lankans. Here, 1,500 people were passing by on a train about half a mile from the ocean. They were swept away by a tidal wave that penetrated that distance and more inland. You can still see photographs of the victims' faces posted along the graveyards by the sea.

You'd never know there had been a tsunami here, however, as the entire coastline has been rebuilt. But owing to the atrocious heat, humidity and bugs of the tropics, many of the new buildings look as weathered and worn as if they've been here for decades.

Just down the road, the ancient port of Galle hosts the largest remaining European fortress in Asia. Thousands of years ago, this was the site of Tarshish, the seaport favored by King Solomon traders, seeking the gold, ivory and spices of Asia.

In 1505, a Portuguese ship sought shelter here from a storm. When the locals refused to let the sailors through their gates, they shot up the town and took it by force. Galle's fortress arose over the next two centuries, overlooking the sea. Back when Portugal ruled this corner of the world, its troops sallied from the stone bastions of the Sun, Moon and Star towers to apprehend passing ships, barring the route to the Orient.

Our swing through Mirissa and Galle is followed by the crush of thousands on the mad streets of the capital at Colombo, where we wade down the sidewalks shoulder-to-shoulder in a stream of sweating humanity. Time to move on.

"I hope you're ready for India," I say to Jeannette as we board a plane heading north. "Sri Lanka is like getting vaccinated for the big show across the water."

"You keep going on with warnings about India," she says. "What's the big deal?"

"When you come back from this trip, everyone will ask you what your favorite country was to visit," I say. "And chances are it will be India, not because it's a 'fun' place, but because it's such a bizarre experience.

"India is like its own planet," I add. "It's the kind of place you tend to love and hate at the same time because it's so strange and chaotic with people piled up all over each other. They have their own pop stars and film scene and way of doing things that we're clueless about. Most of the people living here have probably never heard of Madonna or the Beatles."

"Well now you're being silly," Jeannette says. "Who cares if someone in India doesn't know about Madonna? And when you think of it, most people in America don't know anything about India either. I mean, can you name a single Indian pop star? I can't. Can you name their president? I mean, if they even have one."

"Yeah, you got me there. But what I'm saying is that it's the kind of place that's so alien that it can get to you, no matter how much you've traveled. I've heard of travelers who are so overwhelmed by the crowds, the dirt, the beggars and the hassle that they just cower in their hotel rooms. The woman who wrote 'Eat, Pray, Love' hid out in an ashram the whole time she was here and never even saw India."

"But that's not us," Jeannette says. "You won't see me hiding out in a hotel room. I plan to see as much as I can."

Southern India

Jeannette has her brave face on as we exit the airport in the tongue-twisting town of Thiruvananthapuram and head south on a highway which appears to have a garbage dump down its median. A moraine of crumpled cans, broken glass and plastic bags stretches all down the highway with a cow browsing amid the carnage here and there. Although they may be sacred, the cows of India often die in agony from ingesting this deluge of plastic bags.

Seasoned stoics by now, we endure our taxi driver dodging and weaving through traffic, driving halfway to Kovalam on the wrong side of the center line.

Welcome to India.

Kerala is the unlikely Land of Karl Marx. Communist banners bearing the hammer & sickle along with photos of Lenin, Marx, Fidel Castro and Che Guevera appear along the roadside as a sign that the party of the Workers' Paradise is still popular here in Kerala, the southernmost state of India.

Kerala is India's most prosperous state per capita and has the highest literacy rate in the country, 70 percent, owing to the fact that communism proved to be a big success here when it was introduced in 1957. In fact, Kerala was the first place in the world that communism was freely introduced by popular election, bringing the kind of land reforms and public education that are found nowhere else in India.

But the squalor of the village outside our hotel belies this alleged success: the homes tend toward one-room shacks of rotting wood, gray and black with mold and dirt; the ubiquitous corrugated sheet metal roofs, haphazardly attached; the packed dirt yard without a hint of landscaping; the dark interior inviting swarms of mosquitoes and vermin. A couple of open-air shops offer root vegetables, onions, cheap Indian soft drinks and nameless commodities powdered with dust from the roadway.

"I will not go here at night," our tuk-tuk driver mutters, weaving between ruts and potholes. "Bad people here."

The folks along the road look no worse than the usual lot, but I suppose that if you're a tuk-tuk driver that no one in the neighborhood knows, you're fair game. As for ourselves, Jeannette and I don't feel the least bit threatened.

Here and there we find a few new, well-tended, gated bungalows, a sign of better things to come. And the villagers seem friendly enough; as is the case all over India, they are immaculate in their own grooming and apparel, oblivious to their tragic surroundings.

A fruit seller on the beach offers a platter of pineapple, mangos and bananas. She's dressed in a flowing red and gold sari and a seashell comb rides her raven hair, which is immaculately coiffed and braided above almond eyes. She has golden earrings, a nose ring, and her smile unfolds like a lotus flower from the chocolate depths of her face.

Our next encounter is with a beggar as black and thin as a walking stick with a dirty rag the color of mop water wrapped around his head. He looks liké he's in his 80s, but who knows? Perhaps he has HIV and is younger than us. In any case, a few rupees produce a radiant smile and eyes that sparkle with joy.

Doubting Thomas

A little church just off the beach bears witness to the arrival of the apostle Thomas on the shores of Kerala in 52 A.D. Christianity was established in India long before it took root in Europe.

This was the "Doubting Thomas" of the New Testament, who didn't believe that Jesus had been resurrected. "Unless I see the nail marks in his hands and put my finger where the nails were, and put my hand into his side, I will not believe," he says in the Gospel of John. At a gathering of the apostles, the resurrected Jesus invited Thomas to probe the wounds he suffered during the crucifixion, and of course, Thomas doubted no longer.

Thomas made up for his lapse, sailing to the southern coast of India to establish seven churches in Kerala. At that time there were colonies of Jews along the southern coast of India, connected to the Middle East by a trade route across the sea. Thomas was martyred at Mylapore near Chennai in 72 A.D., but his followers, known as the St. Thomas Christians, carry on in India to this day.

"Check that out," Jeannette says as we wander the beach at sundown.

We see a huge illuminated cross on a hill, blazing with hundreds of lightbulbs. Hundreds of villagers dressed in white are singing hymns on the beach below. Their saris fade from white to red with the setting sun.

Our hotel is located down a long dirt road paralleling the beach just beyond the village. A sign in our room offers this plea: "Please do not wash your clothes in the toilet."

It's lovely, but remote, about 12 miles south of the tourist action at Kovalam Beach, which is reachable only via a jolting ride on a three-wheeled tuk-tuk. The neighboring village is so poverty-stricken it doesn't even have a café. Thus, no restaurants, bars, shops, nada; only all-inclusive, gated hotels line the hills like forts above the beach, filled with tourists hiding out from India. After scrambling along a ridge for two hours, we finally find an expensive vegetarian buffet at one of these tourist prisons.

"I blame these gated hotels for all the B.S. you read in the travel magazines about Kerala," I say while munching on a chapati. "I'll bet they offer travel writers a free stay in return for writing all the happy-talk stories about Kerala that you read in the travel sections."

Because the truth is, coastal Kerala is a kind of a downer. Beyond its all-inclusive hotels, the town of Kovalam Beach swarms with aggressive touts who are in your face at every moment, hawking drums, saris, fruit, maps, cigarettes, statues and such.

"It sounds cruel, but sitting on the beach here feels like you're waving at flies all day," I say. "No, no, no, no..."

Still, back at our remote hotel, we have what is said to be the most beautiful beach in India almost all to ourselves since the British have stayed away in droves this year due to their punk economy. Usually, half of England journeys to India each winter the way Americans flock to Florida.

"Our" beach is a broad frying pan of sand and sun lined with fishing boats stretching south, further than the eye can see.

"There's not much to do here, but at least we can walk the beach," Jeannette says. "We'll get an early start tomorrow and walk 10 miles down and back."

It's a great plan, but early the next morning we head for the beach only to discover that this is where the villagers take their morning dumps, something they've done for thousands of years. Every 100 yards for miles down the beach there's a person squatting by the sea.

"I'll be damned if I'm going to mess up someone's morning crap," I say.

"Or step in it. But I'll miss our walk down the beach," Jeannette says sadly.

Of Goddesses & Gods

Heading out of Thiruvananthapuram, we find the way blocked by a sea of women.

"Look at all the women!" Jeannette says. "There must be thousands of them."

In fact, the streets are lined with tens of thousands of women in lively conversation, squatting on the curbside over containers of their finest dishes.

The taxi driver tells us that this is the day of Karadaiyan Nonbu when the women of southern India worship the goddess Gowri. The women prepare their best recipes as a sacrifice to the goddess in the hope that she will grant long life and protection for their husbands.

"Imagine anything of this sort happening in America," I say as our taxi creeps along.

The festival is based on the tale of a princess named Savithri who saved her husband, Satyavan, from Yama, the god of death.

Yama came upon the couple relaxing in a forest and decided to take the soul of Savithri's husband. But the goddess Gowri gave Savithri the wisdom she needed to confound the Lord of Death with a series of clever arguments, saving her hubby. She talked circles around the devil until he did the equivalent of looking at his watch and claiming he had to be off to another engagement.

At the end of the day, the women have a huge feast on the streets, wrapping up the festival. But for us a more pressing concern is getting to the airport, since every road is blocked with women streaming into town. Somehow our cab driver negotiates a path down a series of alleys, creeping past the endless throng.

No one can beat the Hindus when it comes to goddesses and gods.

They've got either 33 million deities or 333 million, depending on which holy man or source you consult. The Indians seem to get confused on their numbers, and who can blame them with so many gods?

But the point is, the Hindus have gobs of gods, with each one representing a different facet of the human personality, imagination or spirit. If you can imagine a giant flying octopus with supernatural powers and a gift for gab, it could well be as a Hindu god. Thus, the Virgin Mary is also a Hindu goddess, just as Spongebob Squarepants might also rise to godhead in whatever dimension such deities occupy. Toss in Optimus Prime, Bugs Bunny, Wonder Woman, the Canaan god Baal and the Aztec's Quetzalcoatl if you wish; whatever can be imagined is welcome in the Hindu pantheon.

We arrive at the airport with minutes to spare on a flight to Goa, and I fall prey to the opportunistic side of the Indian character. A porter seizes my pack as if it's a requirement of the airport and transports it 50 feet across the lobby to the X-ray machine. Then he extends his palm for a tip. Sighing, I give him 50 rupees, about a dollar.

"It's 100 rupees sir," he whispers, leaning in close. "One hundred rupees."

Bad Behavior

With a number of budget airlines competing for your rupees, it's fairly cheap to fly within the borders of India and a lot less hassle than taking the train. We head north several hundred miles to the old hippie colony at Anjuna on the beach in Goa.

Alas, the days of stringing beads and all-night Goan raves on the beach have been dissolved by the universal solvent of tourism. Now gentrified for the backpacker set, Anjuna looks like a mash-up of a bikers rally and a beer commercial with a long row of bars on stilts running down the coast. The beach is one big party, packed with thousands of tourists, dancing in the bars to trance music beneath the glow of green lasers and flaming fire pots filled with hot coals. Wandering through what passes for a town, several stall merchants ask if we want to buy marijuana, hashish or pills.

It's our kind of place.

"Looks like I've got a new friend," Jeannette says, strolling alongside a huge brahma bull with 20-inch horns in Anjuna's gigantic flea market. It's a weekly Woodstock of crafty commerce that attracts vendors from throughout Asia.

Since we packed next to no clothing for our trip (some shorts and a couple of t-shirts), Jeannette and I have taken to buying new duds as we travel around the world, mailing home the excess when our packs begin to groan. In the market she finds an embroidered skirt which is dotted with tiny mirrors, a necklace (50 rupees), and some silver hoop earrings with semi-precious stones.

On the beach, Jeannette twirls in her new get-up.

"You are so gorgeous, hippie girl."

"I only wish I could bring my friends back here," she says. "They'd love this!"

"I'm sure you'd have a full-blown shopping hurricane."

Although several months of travel have placed us on the scruffy side of things, we can't compete in the freaky looks department with the hipsters who fill the market, including European expats who've lived here as craftspersons for years. They've established workshops with their own clothing and jewelry lines.

A busty German woman in her 50s strolls around the market in a pink tutu, a bare midriff and knee-high cowgirl boots. Elsewhere, the razor-sliced tee shirt is popular, along with waist-length dreads, elaborate tattoos and piercings. Also, skinny is "in." Very in.

There's trouble in paradise, however. Since the Russians started coming to Goa a few years ago, the Brits and other Europeans have stayed away in droves. It seems the Ruskies (a group that includes Ukrainians, Georgians and Kazakhs) have a bad reputation in the manners department and there have been confrontations.

"They don't spend any money," a shopkeeper says. "They just get drunk."

"The Russians are rude, they demand more than you can give; you can make nothing," says another shop owner. "One of them made me pull down every t-shirt in my shop. He agreed on a price and then left without buying."

It's claimed that the Russians have even driven the British from their traditional vacation grounds. This seems a bit disingenuous since the Brits are known throughout the travel world for bad behavior when on "holiday." Word has it that they're so reserved and uptight back home that when they travel abroad they go a bit crazy, up all night drinking, braying and trashing hotel rooms.

But apparently there are levels of obnoxiousness that we are only dimly aware of. On our way to Goa, a Ukrainian tells us that a group of his unruly countrymen were attacked by taxi drivers in the beach town of Palolem. They were clubbed so badly that several had to go to the hospital, one with a fractured skull.

Bad behavior seems to be a global problem for the travel industry. Back in Sri Lanka, our guide, Bruno, said that when he began leading tours of his own country a hotel owner refused him admittance because he was a native. Bruno is as gentlemanly as a choir boy, and in fact, used to be one, but the Sri Lankans are so disorderly that they're not welcome in many hotels in their own homeland. They tend to trash their rooms and disturb other guests.

In fact, we saw "Foreigners Only" signs on a number of hotels there. On our last night in Colombo we endured a steady stream of drunken Sri Lankan tourists yelling out in the hotel hallway from 2:30 a.m. until our wake-up at 4.

For Men Only

A 12-mile hike up and down the beach to the old Portuguese fort of Aguada takes us past thousands of tourists lounging in sun chairs or playing by the sea.

Many of them are young Indian men in their teens or early 20s. Less than one percent (if that) are women. The men stroll along hand-in-hand or dance together in beachside clubs. The beach scene comes across as a massive gay festival.

"Why aren't there any women on the beach?" I ask a waiter.

"The men all take buses here for a holiday," he says.

"Yes, but why aren't there any women?"

"The women are afraid to come," he shrugs, as if the reason is obvious.

At first I think I've misheard him and ask again, "But where are their girlfriends or wives?"

This makes him uncomfortable and he doesn't get where I'm coming from.

"The women, they can't come on the same bus as the men..." he says, leaving off the rejoinder that it wouldn't be safe.

In subsequent news reports of gang rape in India, it's no surprise that native women tend to travel in groups and steer clear of busloads of men. While young Western women think nothing of strolling the beaches of Goa in the merest scraps of bikinis and thongs, the very few Indian women we see here go swimming fully clothed in their saris. They're draped to the point of drowning when they stagger from the sea.

Women, it seems, are excluded from having fun in India. Their job is to stay home with the cooking, cleaning and kids.

The Tree Fort

Goa is a travelers paradise comprised of a neckace of tourist towns ranging for miles up and down the beach. At the center of this scene is the hectic crossroads of Calangute, which attracts Indian tourists from Mumbai in addition to travelers from all over the world.

But, as the saying goes, less is more in Goa, so we make our escape far to the south to blissful Palolem Beach where we find a bamboo beach hut perched 15 feet above the sands on stilts, anchored to a palm tree with some weathered twine.

With no glasses available we perch in our treehouse verandah and enjoy a bottle of Sula, an Indian cabernet that would be considered mouthwash anywhere else. We down it Ernest Hemingway-style out of the bottle as the ball of the sun sinks into the sea.

Palolem Beach spreads in a crescent for a kilometer to the north, fringed with beach bars and rubber-necked palm trees that crane for the sea. Our hut is tied together with twine and finishing nails, with a rickety ladder made of two-by-fours. It cost an exorbitant $24 per night, twice that of the palm-thatched cabanas just off the beach.

Incredibly, it has a sink and a toilet, negating the need to hike down the ladder to an outhouse, where a bucket of water is used in lieu of toilet paper. The toilet wobbles a bit on the rattan floor, so it must be approached gingerly.

"The floor sags so much I hope we don't fall right through it," Jean-nette says.

"Try keeping to the edges."

Despite its saggy floor, we wouldn't trade our digs for a $500-per-night luxury hotel because the view from our hut is of a little Nirvana, taking in two square miles of a tropical utopia, as if we've arrived in a place that only Gulliver might stumble upon.

"People come here planning to spend three days and end up staying three or four months," one of our new British friends tells us in the beach bar downstairs.

On the other hand, we'll definitely be nesting in our silk sleep sacks tonight, because the foam rubber mattress and sheet are on par with what you'd expect in a leper colony. The backpacking adventure includes being mindful of bed bugs.

Part of the scenery here includes two gorgeous, well-endowed Russian girls, about 19 years old, lolling in the sun chairs next to us. They're wearing the merest bits of colored string when they're not topless. They might as well be in the nude. It's all I can do to lock my gaze in the other direction while Jeannette sits, bemused, reading her book.

Later, the girls frolic on the beach in their thongs, throwing a frisbee with several young Indian waiters. I marvel that the lads don't have erections as long as Pinocchio's nose; perhaps they have yogic powers of concentration.

I spared Jeannette the agony of taking five local buses to get here and hired a driver, Harish, who we met back in Anjuna. Hiring a driver is a quintessentially Indian thing to do.

"Do you like driving?" Jeannette asks.

"Oh yes," he says. "I was a bartender on the beach for five years before I started driving. Sometimes I had to work 24 hours a day. At Christmas and the New Year I would get only three or four hours of sleep and then have to go back to the bar."

Working nonstop through one's waking hours seems to be the norm across Asia, where the leisure time we Westerners take for granted is an unknown commodity.

"I like driving a taxi because I can rest between runs," Harish says. "I can pull over and sleep."

"Do you own this taxi?"

"No, but I am saving. I can buy this car new at a cost of $8,000."

Sunita's Story

Jeannette makes friends with Sunita, a young woman who owns the shop filled with dresses, earrings and trinkets below our tree fort. Sunita is 24 and the mother of five children through an arranged marriage when she was 16. They all live in a single room around the back of the hotel-bar where we're staying, making due with the communal shower and the outhouse that serves as the customers' toilet.

Sunita began working on the beach when she was 11 years old and has been running her shop since the age of 14. She speaks fair English, which she learned entirely on her own from conversing with tourists; yet she doesn't know how to read or write, not even her name.

Sunita is at her small stall from before we wake up in the morning until 10:30 at night.

"I haven't had a sale in two days, but still I must pay my rent," she tells Jeannette. It's the fate of 1,000 tourist shop owners in Goa, who all sell the same statuettes of dancing Shiva, carved elephants and mirrored knick-knacks with little result.

"Please come look at my shop. Just look, no buy," she begs. After promising several times, Jeannette makes good for a pedicure, a henna tattoo and a pair of earrings.

"Why do the Hindu gods have so many arms?" Jeannette asks while getting her tattoo.

"It's because they... how do I say? Each arm means the god has a special power," Sunita says. "When one arm holds a flute, it means he is a musician; when another holds a sword it means he is a man of war. For woman gods, the arms might show that she is a healer, or can help bring babies, or with the planting."

Over the next few days Sunita has Jeannette wrapped around her little finger, making sale after sale with her puppy dog eyes.

"The sad thing is she's probably one of the more prosperous businesswomen in Goa," I say.

"Well, she really does know how to hustle," Jeannette says.

Sunita's husband was crushed when his wife delivered her fourth girl; they have only one son. As is the case all over the developing world, baby girls tend to be bad news.

This is because a son is charged with being the family breadwinner when he grows up, whereas a girl runs the risk of getting pregnant as a teen, a disaster for her aging parents. And in India, a daughter's parents must also pay a hefty dowry to the groom's family when it's time to marry. This can amount to tens of thousands of dollars if the young man has a promising career, such as a software engineer in Bangalore.

Thus, Sunita and her husband know they must bear the expense of four dowries in the years ahead, and possibly, domestic disaster if their girls get pregnant out of wedlock.

Yet paradoxically, women control the finances of their families in India. It tends to be a grandmother's role to decide what gets spent and when. Sunita clearly calls the shots in her family; her husband mostly mopes around in the background.

Sunita stands in the blazing sun in front of her shop all day long and into the night, begging people to "come look, take a look, just look." She grovels for tourists who spend more on beer than she makes in a day, possibly more than she makes in a week.

When Westerners think of mantras, "Om" springs to mind, but in India, it's "come look, just look my friend" that's repeated the most often.

The Master

Each morning a deeply tanned and silver-haired yoga master who looks to be in his 70s conducts a class on the beach outside our hut. He lives in a cave up in the rocks and leads his classes almost naked, wearing only a leather g-string with a small flap over his genitals. A beautiful young blonde in a blue bikini with waist-length hair is his companion.

As lean and muscled as a bullwhip, the yogi finishes his classes each day with a swim straight out of sight into the ocean doing the butterfly stroke, the most difficult and strenuous form of swimming.

"Don't you think there must be sharks out there, and jellyfish?" Jeannette says.

"He's got to be the bravest man alive," I say, awestruck.

"He must use yoga to conquer fear."

"I can't even begin to imagine."

We watch in silence as the yogi's catapulting arms carry him out of sight in the distant waves. He utterly disappears into the boundless horizon of the Indian Ocean.

"We've timed him," says one of the Brits in the bar. "He swims for five-and-a-half hours each day, straight out to the horizon and back."

Lucky are those able to practice yoga in India, for here in its birthplace this unification of body, mind and spirit is vibrant with power and meaning.

Even in rural northern Michigan, Jeannette and I know many young women who've made the yoga pilgrimage to India, studying to be teachers at ashrams in Pune, Mysore, Kerala and the foothills of the Himalayas.

The precursors of yoga are hinted at in contortionist sculptures dating back more than 3,000 years, but the first time the practice was written about was in the scriptures of the Upanishads, 300 years before Christ.

No one knows for sure what the word "yoga" means. In ancient India it was the root of the words "to yoke," "war chariot" and "to concentrate." Today, yoga is popularly held to mean "union," that of the body, mind and soul.

American men have their own translation. "Yoga is womens' revenge exercise," according to a male friend back home. "Women can bend in ways that men can only dream of."

But such is not the case in India where yoga is traditionally practiced only by men. And it was male yogis who developed its various disciplines. Perhaps Indian men are more rubbery than their American cousins, or more willing to bend.

Personally, the meaning of yoga means "a journey" to me because I've endeavored for years to do the standing postures balanced on one foot without much success. I can manage a fair semblance of Standing Tree pose after a decade of trying, but the trickier postures, such entwining my arms and legs in a Full Eagle are, as mentioned, still a journey.

Yoga was popularized in the West starting in the late 1800s when Guri Vivekananda brought the practice to the World Columbian Exposition in Chicago in 1893. Vivekananda also helped revive the Hindu religion in India, bringing its millions of gods to the attention of citizens in the U.S. and Britain during several years of lecture tours.

His foothold was followed by the work of B.K.S. Iyengar. Born into poverty and suffering from tuberculosis, Iyengar began studying yoga at the age of 13 in the early 1900s at a time when it had been largely forgotten in India. He went on to publish "Light on Yoga," a manual which kicked off the hatha yoga movement in the West that snow-balled in the 1980s. Today, more than 20 million Americans practice yoga, including Jeannette and me.

Almost forgotten, Hinduism and yoga. Odd that these ancient teachings resurfaced in an age when we are all but slaves to technology.

The Bumpy Bus

With a case of Buddha Belly coming on and frequent explosive trips to the bathroom (which, like most tropical potties has no toilet seat), I nonetheless decide to go ahead with our plan to visit the ancient ruins of Hampi, about 160 miles inland.

Bad idea.

We catch a midnight sleeper bus and land a crib directly above the rear axle. There are no shocks on the bus, so we are jackhammered up and down the entire way, a trip of more than six hours.

I've learned from past trips to pack along a supply of the bowel sup-pressant Imodium for emergencies. It works for awhile, but around 2:30 in the morning I'm part of the chorus begging the bus to stop. What I've got comes on like a mudslide in a matter of seconds. We pile out of the bus by the side of the road in the pitch blackness and I make my mark on India with a gushing splash. "Be careful where you walk!" I call out, as if anyone could see shit, so to speak.

Jeannette has a dream on the bus that takes her faraway home.

"Wow, aggressive snow plow drivers chase me," she writes in our blog. "Grinding gears, plowing over and into everything. No! It won't get me, I duck into an alley. Three roads over, I wait, lights out. Breathe in and out, over and over. Listen. Rrrrr... grinding gears. NO! Wait, wait. Closer..."

Guess the night was rough for her, too. By the time we reach the hurly-burly of Hospet, a modern city outside the ruins, I feel almost comatose, unable to grasp what the touts are saying. I wave them away, their faces swimming before my eyes, but they come back and back, plugging places to stay in town.

Eventually, too sick to protest any longer, I surrender to a tuk-tuk driver who goes by the name of Black Cobra. He takes us to his family's guesthouse where we land a room for $8 per night. Black Cobra runs the place with his brother, Dragon Cobra. He enlists himself to guide us through the miles of ruins in his tuk-tuk.

Their names are so goofy that I decide on the spot that my own travel name will be Black Dragon to go with my initials. (This idea goes nowhere and is soon forgotten.)

Jeannette's travel name is Pashmina, after the cashmere material woven from the fine hairs found on the underbelly of goats, which is hawked everywhere in Asia. Most of the time, this alleged pashmina is nothing more than polyester.

But everywhere we go shopkeepers call out to Jeannette, "Pashmina! Pashmina! Madame, do you want pashmina?"

Black Cobra wheels us around Hampi, pointing out a colossal stable that once housed hundreds of elephants used for warfare, construction and transportation.

With me being sick, Jeannette guides me through the ruins like an invalid. I hope Lord Krishna, the cowboy god, has a sense of humor and compassion, because I made an impromptu mess in the dusty debris of one of his ruined temples. But then, one of his 333 million buddy gods gave me the craps after all, so please return to sender.

Some 700 years ago, Hampi was known throughout the world as a trading center for diamonds, gold and gems. Some 18 miles in circumference, this huge city was an adjunct of the Silk Road, which runs hundreds of miles to the north. There are still carvings of traders from China, Russia, the Mideast and Greece on its walls amid thousands of sculptures.

We often think of Marco Polo as history's lone traveler to the Far East, but gazing upon these bas reliefs of traders from all over the known world, it's apparent that there must have been thousands of people bouncing back and forth between Europe and Asia.

"It boggles the mind that traders from Russia and Europe traveled all the way to southern India hundreds of years ago," I say. But Jeannette seems quite unboggled by this revelation.

Today, Hampi is a dusty desert of a place, filled with hundreds of temples and palaces, bone-dry and hot as hell, but beautiful in its desolation.

We rise at dawn and follow an elephant down to the river on a path of flagstones laid 500 years ago. Here, we find villagers taking baths beneath their saris and slapping their laundry on boulders the size of trucks that fill the riverbed. A shepherd marches a herd of goats along the dirt road and elsewhere a line of brahma cattle saunter past travelers from around the world. The best show in town is watching the temple elephant stroll down to the river twice a day for his bath.

We have an ugly incident with a street peddler in Hampi, typical of the kind of hassles that travelers encounter in the developing world. While sitting in a tuk-tuk, I make the mistake of expressing a passing interest in a wooden flute. In the West, this means you're simply curious about something, "just looking." But in the developing world, the slightest sort of interest means you're in a serious negotiation, which must end with a sale.

The aggressive young vendor won't take no for an answer, so it quickly turns into an angry pissing match with me "standing on principle."

"No, no, not interested," I say over and over again, getting increasingly angry as the argument drags on. "I don't want it." But he refuses to listen. Finally, he throws the flute in my lap, as if to say, "You're stuck with it buddy." This too is a common practice around the world.

I quickly place the flute on the ground, whereupon his eyes fly wide open and his mouth drops in what looks like the shock of a lifetime. And though I've won the battle of the toy flute, I feel like a prick as our tuk-tuk pulls away.

"I should have just bought his goddamn flute, but that would be rewarding bad behavior," I say.

"Talk about bad karma," Jeannette says.

Unfortunately, desperate street peddlers around the world tend to use this same technique, refusing to take no for an answer in the hope of wearing you down. I don't know if anyone has ever been killed for refusing to buy a trinket worth a dollar or two, but I've endured some hate-filled glares that seemed a whisker away from murder.

That night, Black Cobra asks if we'd like to go on a beer run. Sure, what the hell. Hampi is one of India's irritating "sacred cities," where no booze is allowed, but we can buy some in Hospet and sneak it into our hotel. Mum's the word.

We take Black Cobra's tuk-tuk to a stark bar along a darkened road. It's not a bar as we know it, but more of a shabeen, a bare bones drinking room without tables or chairs. I buy three quarts of beer through a hole in the wall, including one for Black Cobra.

Black Cobra instructs Jeannette to wait outside in the tuk-tuk. Going inside I can see why because the bar is packed with a rough mob of Indian men in a rowdy party mode with not a woman in sight. There's never been a woman in this dump and never will be. It would take a buzz saw to cut through the machismo in this place.

It occurs to me that my blond bombshell has been told to wait outside in the dark not just because this is no place for a lady, but for her own safety. Shit! I scurry out the door, relieved to find her peeping from the shadows of the tuk-tuk.

The Beer Bash

We check out the Indian nightlife scene on our last night in Goa, catching a party boat out of Panjim, the state capital.

When the Portuguese landed in Goa in the early 1500s, Panjim became the gateway to trade with Asia. They held onto Goa and their slice of India for 450 years. It wasn't until 1961 that independent India annexed this treasure.

At the dock in town, a triple-decker cruise boat is packed bum-to-bum with excited locals, chattering like a flock of lorikeets. The Indian women are gorgeous in their rainbow saris and salwar pajama suits in colors of poppy, cornflower, scarlet, emerald and gold, some as luscious as the bubble-breasted goddess Parvati.

"So, women in India do get to have fun after all," Jeannette says, recalling the female-free beach at Calangute.

"Yeah, but they've got to put up with Indian men to do so," I note.

More than a few of the men onboard are staggering drunk and lugging liters of beer around in pursuit of getting more so. One of these merrymakers has dark, devil eyes, leering and pawing at women passing by. I steer blondie in the other direction.

"Don't look at him," I say. "The worst thing you can do with a combative drunk is to catch his eye."

But Mr. Rowdy is so blasted that he trips over his own feet and tumbles sideways to the deck, where he is quickly carried away by a quartet of bouncers.

"Looks like they're used to this sort of thing," Jeannette says as the party swirls on around us.

"These guys sure can't hold their beer," I say, thinking of the capacity of my friends back home. But then, we're a bunch of drunken old goats who've had much more practice imbibing.

The Man With No Arms

India is a fairly easy place to get around, and a few days later we find ourselves gliding into the capital at Delhi.

"I've never wanted to go to northern India," I say as our taxi flows with the current of traffic into town. "Other travelers have told me it's the poorest, dirtiest and most overpopulated part of the country. Even the hard-core backpackers say it's a bummer."

"I guess we're going to find out for ourselves," Jeannette says. "Look over there."

We see a toddler girl, perhaps three years old, sitting naked by a fountain with no adult in sight to keep an eye on her as the river of traffic steams by. Her mother materializes from around the bend to give her a bath. Just another day in Delhi, it seems.

Traffic is the curse of India's prosperity. Delhi is awash in the endless, satanic roar of honking horns and a steel mesh of automobiles, tuk-tuks, motorbikes and trucks jostling five abreast on a three-lane road. We pass a slum neighborhood that looks as if it's held together with spit and gravity, homes made up of a mish-mash of plastic bags and cardboard boxes.

And yet, I don't see large numbers of people living on the street as was the case in Mumbai a few years back; they're surely here, but not on the route we went down. And as elsewhere in India, there seems to be a breath of prosperity in the air.

Delhi is considered more of a passing-through point than a destination for many travelers, but we take a crack at it, plunging into the dense soup of humanity that bubbles through the old part of town. We visit the Red Fort, built by the Mughal rulers of India back in the 1500s; its walls run for several miles in circumference. Blond Jeannette draws stares from men and women alike. She's as rare as fairy dust here.

We get the quintessential Delhi crowd experience, riding the metro train around town with passengers jammed together as tight as a pack of cigarettes, albeit a soggy one, slippery with the sweat of hundreds of bodies, owing to the temperature of 106 degrees Fahrenheit. Jeannette rides in the women-only car, protection against getting groped or worse.

We also spend an afternoon on the more typical side of life in Delhi, walking up and down a mile-long commercial market among tens of thousands of Indian shoppers. Since there's no tourist junk here and few Westerners, we don't suffer from the hassle that's routine at temples and other tourist spots. The shop owners leave us alone, and we have the refreshing experience of being able to look through their goods without a hard sell.

Later, a young man chases me through the market with his arms outstretched. Both of them have been cut off at the elbows.

"Sir? Hullo? Sir? Sir?"

The armless man's sudden appearance is like a waking nightmare. I turn my back on him and flee down the street in terror.

A couple hours later I bump into him again.

"How did you lose your arms?"

"It was an accident."

"An auto accident?"

"It's a long list," he says, leaving me to wonder at this enigmatic answer.

I stick a bill in his shirt pocket and look at him a little closer. He is well dressed and fairly well filled out. But it's not the kind of gig anyone would voluntarily choose, even at the bottom of the heap in Delhi. For all we know, his arms were cut off by the local mafia when he was a child to use him as a beggar slave.

Down the Ganges

We hook up with another band of backpackers and take an overnight train to the Ganges River, traveling second-class in a three-tiered sleeper car. This is a cubicle measuring six-by-seven feet square, with three steel bunks on either side stacked to the ceiling. You chain your pack under the bed, get cozy with your neighbors, and sleep in your clothes, thankful that you're not one of the hundreds of people sitting up all night long on wooden benches in the third class cars.

At Mirzapur, the legendary Ganges shines like a mirror in the morning sun, but fades to the color of snot-green the closer we get. This is the holy river of India, where pilgrims come to wash away their sins.

A dead goat floats in a gumbo of algae, trash and soap bubbles just a splash away from where kids are swimming and women are washing their clothes. Next to them are the wrecks of several small fishing boats.

The Ganges has its source in the glaciers of the Himalayas, but in Hindu mythology it springs from the head of Shiva, the dancing God of Destruction and Rebirth.

We're a bit shocked to learn that the battered wooden rowboats floating in the green goop aren't wrecks. In fact, they are going to be our home for the next three days as we float 60 miles downriver to India's holiest city, Varanasi. Each has a spindly bamboo mast, a faded cotton sail, and a tattered vinyl tarp for protection from the sun.

All day we float down the river, paddled by villagers who've developed this trip as a family business. Their oars consist of boards nailed to lengths of bamboo. I take a turn at the oars and find that my lily white man's palms are burned raw within an hour of pulling on the rough bamboo. By contrast, the boat boy's palms are as leathery as baseball gloves. He looks to be about 16 and pulls at the oars all day long.

Our companions make up a mini United Nations, including a brother and sister from New Zealand who are traveling for a year around the world; two single women from California and South Africa, respectively; and a couple engaged to be married, she from South Africa and he from Norway. The latter have recently spent a year living in Australia.

The river ranges up to a mile wide and winds through a flat desert of dusty white plains that seem as desolate as Mars. For a "holy" river it's a godforsaken place with few people and virtually no other boats. The reason for this is because the Ganges floods each year and expands its width for several miles; thus only a very few villages blessed with the occasional hilltop are found on its banks.

We stop at one village, perched atop a high bank; perhaps this refuge becomes an island when the Ganges floods.

The village looks like it was once a thriving place with a cobblebrick walkway and homes of mud bricks and cinderblocks. But virtually every building is riven with cracks or gaping holes and the roofs of corrugated metal or palm thatch are a shambles, meant more to keep out the sun than the rain. A cow peers out from the shadows of one home, gazing at passersby through a wall of tumbled bricks.

The only sign of commerce is a hole-in-the-wall barber shop where a solitary man is having his chin scraped with a straight-edge razor. Otherwise, there are a few women scattered around, as thin as sparrows, peeking shyly through the folds of their saris. One woman squats in the villager square, pounding grain with a stick. With no electricity and a litter of rocks and trash scattered everywhere along its lanes, the village looks more like a ruin than a habitable place. When several of our party asks if there are any toilet facilities, we are directed to the concealment of a tree, just past the huts.

Nonetheless, we find a group of smiling, uniformed children standing at recess outside a large, well-constructed school on the outskirts. It's clearly the finest building in the area and the pride of the town. There are also many large trees in and around the village offering shade in what is otherwise a desert - always a good sign. The people are thin, but no one looks hungry or in search of a hand-out, and we are met with smiles and curiosity.

At night we camp beneath the stars on the riverbank, dining on curried potatoes, rice, chapatis, jackfruit and spinach with cottage cheese. For drink there is chai, a blend of tea, buffalo milk and spices.

Only a few dozen Westerners make this trip each year and we feel blessed to be among them, even though, or especially because, the conditions of this trip haven't changed in thousands of years.

"We've got just an old wooden boat with a puff of wind now and then to fill a ragged sail," Jeannette says as we creep along.

"And has anyone else ever played the American blues on the Ganges at sunrise?" I respond. That morning I had performed the Robert Johnson classic "Rollin' and Tumblin'" with my mini guitar while the sun came up in a ball of fire.

I've been scanning the river for white bundles as we drifted along.

"If you keep an eye out, you'll see bodies floating down the river," I tell Jeannette, confident of the widespread reports I've heard of Indians wrapping their deceased loved-ones in shawls and dumping them in the sacred river for a float to the sea.

"That's not true," says Animesh, the leader of our expedition. "I've never seen a body."

"Really? I expected to see lots of bodies," I say, conjuring memories from an old National Geographic magazine.

Animesh shakes his head no, more vehemently than the usual Indian head wiggle. "I've been doing this trip every three weeks for the past six years and have never seen a body," he says.

"We saw some dead cows, but that's it," Jeannette says. "I guess you never really know what's true until you go and see for yourself."

Mad for Cricket

It's on the Ganges that Jeannette and I are introduced to the mysteries of cricket, a form of baseball which we've seen people playing everywhere on our trip.

Playing with the boat boys, we bean a few balls into the dust of the vast Gangetic floodplain which will be underwater during the monsoon season a few weeks hence.

Everyone is mad for cricket on this side of the world, with up to 100,000 spectators filling stadiums from Australia to Pakistan; yet it seems a ridiculous game until you actually play it.

A bowler gets a running start and makes a windmill pitch at the batman at the plate. The batman gets to hit the ball as many times as he can until he's struck out. This can take hours; some games have reportedly gone on for five straight days.

You can play cricket at any skill level, and it strikes me that the game would make a fine import to the U.S. Worth noting, the Ozzies think that American baseball is a sissy game like something they call rounders. They can't understand why we play it.

The Sacred City

The New Zealand kids spend the boat trip lying immobile in the fetal position as a result of contracting India's notorious amoeboid illness. They ate some particularly noxious looking goop at a market stall back in old Delhi that Jeannette and I wisely passed up. We've learned on many trips that there's always someone (usually young and inexperienced) who's willing to take a chance on eating some exotic foodstuff that's patently horrible. Days, or even weeks, of excruciating sickness are the price.

Fortunately, there's a broad river to throw up in.

Jeannette and I take a pass on bathing in the Ganges, the shores of which smell like excrement the closer we get to Varanasi. But I hazard washing my legs in its slime to claim a partial experience of holy immersion.

"Was it worth it?" Jeannette asks.

"Not really. My legs feel all scummy."

On the third day in the rowboat, we arrive at Varanasi, the sacred city of Lord Shiva and home to five million people. Here are the ghats, stone staircases leading down to the river where Hindus burn the bodies of their dead on wooden pyres, spreading the ashes on the waters of the Ganges.

We even have a welcoming party as our group of nine walks into town with our packs: a long line of beggars with their hands out.

Among the Pilgrims

In the morning we take a boat ride at dawn past the ghats which run for about seven miles along the banks of Varanasi. Crowds of people gather at the Ganges; we see women washing their clothes along the steps while kids splash in the river.

It's said that many people drink this water, which is only a couple of miles downstream from an open sewer pouring shit and piss into the river. We see pilgrims immersing themselves in the water, ecstatic with the prospect of washing away their sins.

Animesh says the host of a TV science show once got the bright idea to drink a cupful of the river water as the locals do. He ended up spending a couple of weeks in the hospital.

The main thing to do in age-old Varanasi is simply to wander for miles along the ghats.

"This is fun, but also kind of an obstacle course," Jeannette says as we dodge beggars and touts along the way. One reeking area is covered with human excrement on a platform well above the river; at least 200 piles. It must pass for some sort of public toilet.

Our companion up and down the ghats is Jenny, a pretty woman in her 50s from South Africa, who is traveling solo in India. She's one of a number of women we've met whose mates don't care to go vagabonding, so they bravely go it alone.

"My husband doesn't care to travel," Jenny says. "He's afraid that our home will get broken into if he leaves."

"South Africa seems to have a reputation for that," I say, adding that we once met a couple who had their entire apartment cleaned out in Capetown, including even their family photos.

"Have you ever thought of moving?" Jeannette asks.

"No, we love it there and live in a lovely town," Jenny says, adding that she makes periodic trips to England to visit family in addition to other trips around the world.

Jeannette and I spent three weeks in South Africa a couple of years back and I found it to be a frightening place populated by a few "haves" enjoying the highest standard of living in the world, surrounded by an ocean of "have-nots" living in concrete huts and surviving on grain provided by the government. In South Africa's so-called Wild Coast, we drove through areas filled with thousands of these dismal huts, with barely a sign of commerce anywhere. It seemed like a vast, rural refugee camp, spreading for hundreds of miles. Mostly, we saw reed-thin women hiking for miles down towering slopes, carrying plastic buckets of water on their heads back uphill to their hovels.

At the time of our trip, the incidence of violence, home invasions and gang rape in South Africa was so high that the country was rated only a notch or two below Iraq in terms of its hazards. For me, the paranoia there was palpable, a shadow that came and went amid the pleasures of South Africa's game parks and wine country.

But obviously, Jenny is more knowledgeable about her home turf than a scaredy-cat tourist passing through. And, worth noting, many

Europeans, Australians and South Africans are afraid to visit the United States, which is also considered one of the most dangerous countries in the world.

We pass the funeral sites, where towering piles of wood are stacked as high as houses on the riverbank. A kiln-like crematorium at one site still has faint traces of smoke where someone's loved one has been incinerated alongside the river; the ashes will be scattered on the water as a final blessing. Behind the crematorium is a hospice where dying people wait their turn at the funeral pyre.

It's a grim and gloomy place, projecting the cloying stench of death, with photos strictly forbidden to offer some slight measure of dignity from gawking tourists. The stacks of wood offer the only color in a scheme of blackened walls and ash gray. It seems almost like an industrial site, not the spiritual sendoff you might imagine. More like the image conjured by the term, charnel house.

But it's claimed that if a Hindu dies in Varanasi, he or she won't have to continue on through the cycles of reincarnation, but will get a free ticket to paradise.

"It makes you wonder why three-fourths of India doesn't move here to skip the misery of existence, not to mention the risk of being reincarnated as a monkey or a cow," I say.

"They probably can't afford to," Jeannette says, "and there are enough people here already."

"People don't really believe in their religions anyway, do they?" I say. "If they did, Christians would be throwing huge parties before they die, anticipating all of the good times they'll be having in heaven with all of the friends and family they'll be seeing again. They'd be thrilled with the idea of dying."

"Don't ask me," she says. "I've never believed in religion."

"You've never been one for all of that New Age stuff either. It's one of the things I like about you," I say, neglecting to mention that I sort of enjoy hippie-dippy talk about reincarnation, chakras and such.

Animesh tells us that the Hindus believe that the human body is made up of five elements: earth, water, wind, fire and a life-giving force called aether. Cremation returns these elements to the universe in the cycle of reincarnation.

"Spreading the ashes on the Ganges brings peace to the dead and also serves a practical purpose," he says. "The ashes contain potassium and phosphorus, which enrich the soil downstream, continuing the cycle of life."

Later that night, we see five bodies burning on pyres by the river. The fires seem both poignant and proud; the spirits of the departed are willing their bodies back to the universe while going out in a blaze of glory.

The center of old Varanasi is jammed with thousands of pilgrims, most of them in traditional dress of gauzy pajamas and turbans. Groups of sadhus stroll toward their temples in their orange robes, with ashes and ritual paint markings on their foreheads. These are men who've given up all of their possessions to live the spiritual life. Some are quite hefty guys, however, so the spiritual life apparently side-steps self-denial.

We brush past a herd of water buffalo wandering down the street near our Israeli-owned hotel and take a bicycle rickshaw a couple of miles downtown, swimming through a crowd which is shoulder-to-shoulder with lines of cows, motorbikes, rickshaws and the occasional automobile, all with a tremendous din of honking horns.

Hilarious, exhilarating, mind-blowing, there aren't enough adjectives in the dictionary to describe the sensations that sweep through us as we wriggle our way through this crowded street and its alleyways, which likely haven't changed a lick in centuries.

"Be careful where you step," I say a few hours later at the temple of Hanuman the Monkey God, promptly planting my bare foot in some monkey crap.

Fortunately, it's on the dry side.

Hanuman is an interesting character in the Hindu pantheon of the gods. He's a giant, invincible monkey, both wise and mischievous, who serves as a lieutenant to Lord Rama, the great hero of Indian mythology.

Swift as the wind, or even the mind itself, Hanuman can't be killed with any weapon. He has the power to inspire fear in his enemies (those sharp teeth, perhaps), can shift shapes at will, and is immune to sexual temptation.

All that, and he has an army of monkey soldiers at his temple in Varanasi, laying traps for barefooted tourists.

The Visitors

"Benares is older than history, older than tradition, older even than legend and looks twice as old as all of them put together."

- Mark Twain, on his 1895 trip to India

The likes of Jesus, Buddha, Mark Twain and Allan Ginsburg all have Varanasi in common.

Or so it's said. They all walked the streets of Varanasi back when it was known as Benares, which claims to be the oldest continuously-occupied city on earth.

Mark Twain came to Benares because he was broke. In the 1890s, Twain invested his fortune in an early version of the typewriter and lost it all. He lost all of his friends' money too, and to make good he decided to write a book about traveling around the world. *Following the Equator* was published in 1897. Twain also pushed on to Sri Lanka, a place he found "unspeakably hot."

We think of Allan Ginsburg as the Beat poet who wrote *Howl*. But Ginsburg was also an intrepid backpacker who traveled to obscure corners of Peru, Africa and Asia decades ahead of other travelers. On one occasion, he landed in Mombassa, Kenya, with $5 in his pocket. In India, he and his companion stayed in such squalid digs that the local police stopped by to investigate what two Westerners were doing in such a pesthole.

Ginsburg spent a year in India in 1964, most of it in Varanasi, where he spent weeks on end smoking hashish and ganja with the saddhus and gazing into the flaming funeral pyres, hoping to learn something about death and rebirth. He returned to San Francisco with the fashions of long hair, Indian clothes, love beads and Eastern ideas that inspired the hippie movement, changing America forever.

So if your redneck cousin Lou still has hair halfway down his back and wears a skull ring a doo-rag and a necklace, it all gets back to Ginsburg and the freaky fashions of the holy men of Varanasi.

Buddha preached his first sermon here 2,500 years ago, but far more interesting is the belief that Jesus spent six years in Varanasi as a young man, followed by six years in the monasteries of Tibet.

In the late 1800s, texts from the second century A.D. were found at a monastery in the Himalayan kingdom of Lhasa, which claimed that Jesus had followed the Silk Road to India at the age of 14. The texts claimed that he was a reincarnation of Buddha, explaining why the three wise men were searching for him in the Mideast.

According to the book, *Jesus Lived in India*, by German theologist/adventurer Holger Kersten, young Jesus reportedly spent his early years in India studying the peaceful tenets of Buddhism, along with yoga and ayurvedic healing. He returned to Palestine at the age of 30, where Kersten claims he conducted numerous "miracles" based on Eastern medicine.

It's not such a far-fetched idea because Hebrew merchants were well established in southern India more than 2,000 years ago, and trade caravans were commonplace between India and the Mideast. Since there's a biblical gap in the life of Jesus from the age of 12 to 30, perhaps he joined a caravan to the east.

Kersten claims that yogic techniques and Eastern medicine allowed Jesus to survive crucifixion. He cites ancient accounts which claim that Jesus eventually traveled to Kashmir, the "Promised Land" of the Bible, where he lived into his 80s and was renowned as a great holy man.

Today, the reputed Tomb of Jesus can still be found in the city of Srinagar in Kashmir. It's also claimed that his mother Mary's tomb is on the border of Pakistan, but these sites are among several claiming that distinction, spreading all the way to Jerusalem.

Still, Kashmir seems a likely place to put on one's bucket list.

The Taj

"I've never cared whether or not I made it to the Taj Mahal, but now that we're here at least we can claim we've been to another of the Great Wonders of the World," I say as we alight from a 13-hour train trip to Agra. Once again, our compartment has six bunks, stacked three to the ceiling on each side.

The Great Wall, Macchu Picchu, Angkor Wat, the Pyramids, Parthenon, Eiffel Tower, Ayers Rock... these are among the wonders of the tourist world, yet it always seemed like a journey to the Taj wouldn't be worth the bother.

But the Taj Mahal is a lotus flower much larger and more beautiful than we expected, solemnly grand in all-white marble. We stroll the impeccable garden grounds for a couple of hours, taking it in from different angles as the sun goes down. Even the Indian tourists are respectful, declining to litter its well-tended grounds.

Our party causes an uproar at its gate because Jeannette and fellow traveler Rachelle of San Francisco have scarves bearing the likenesses of the Hindu gods Shiva and Ganesh - strictly forbidden in a Muslim shrine. These are stuffed away for the sake of religious harmony.

There's a romantic legend about the maharajah who built the Taj as a mausoleum for his third and most beloved wife. As a young man, he used to disguise himself as a woman so he could wander around a ladies-only market unobserved. One day, he espied the beauty who would bear him 14 children. She died during the course of her last childbirth and thus, the Taj was built in her honor over the course of many years.

Unfortunately, its construction drained the state treasury and got folks to grumbling. The heartsick maharajah was imprisoned by his third son, who killed his two older brothers in order to seize the throne. The people approved of the coup because, as the new maharajah pointed out, his father had gone overboard on building the Taj.

The old man never got to visit his creation. He slowly went blind and spent his final days straining to see the Taj, several miles distant from the palace room that became his prison.

Land of the Litter Bug

As for Agra, it comes across as the "City of Open Sewers," a dreadfully smelly place. There's an open sewer, ripe with excrement and urine, running alongside our row of tourist hotels that has us gagging uncontrollably as we walk to and from a restaurant.

"You wouldn't think they'd have a sewer like this right in the hotel area," Jeannette says.

"It's like running a gauntlet," I say as we hold our breath and jog to our hotel.

"Well don't fall in!" she laughs.

Tramping through the dust and filth of northern India each day takes its toll. We've taken to washing our blackened sandals in the shower each night, and our inky feet always need a good scrubbing. Blow your nose and the tissue comes out black after a day of tramping around.

"They just don't seem to notice all the trash lying around," I say of the Indians. "I don't think they have a clue as to how dirty their country is compared to the rest of the world."

"Well, after a couple of weeks you do start to forget it's there," Jeannette says.

A British traveler gives us the lowdown on why the Indians are immaculate in their personal hygiene and clothing, yet contemptuous of their surroundings.

"I went sailing with some young Indian fellows and saw them throwing their bottles and trash all over the beach and into the sea," he says. "When I asked them why they didn't pick up their trash, they said it was because they didn't want to put a beach cleaner out of work."

"That sounds like a cop-out," I say, thinking of all of the anti-littering messages I've seen posted on poles and buildings in India.

"Yes, but down in the villages where most people are illiterate, no one would dream of cleaning up the trash because that's considered a low-caste job that's beneath their dignity."

Also disturbing in India are the number of child beggars and mothers begging with their babies. In Varanasi we saw naked toddlers and infants rolling around on the blackened sidewalks where people have been spitting and cows shitting, all with mamma sitting in the dirt with her hand out.

"Why have a baby in the first place if you can't take care of it, or if your child's fate is to be an illiterate beggar, not much above the state of an animal?" I wonder.

"Maybe those moms are asking themselves the same thing," Jeannette says.

A country packed with 1.2 billion people and no 'off' switch on its population is sure to have its troubles. Agra lies in Uttar Pradesh, the most populous state in India with 200 million people crammed into an area the size of New England.

Uttar Pradesh is a population bomb disaster. Yet how can the Indians help but reproduce far beyond what's reasonable? There's virtually nothing to do in their godforsaken villages except getting laid as relief from the boredom of existence; and when it's hot, people like to have sex even more. It's plenty hot in India.

It's been suggested that bringing television to the villages of India would help reduce the country's population because gazing at the tube would provide an alternative to having sex.

For our part, we're happy to have experienced Uttar Predesh. It's been like traveling to another planet. But we're also happy to leave its crowds behind. It's time to move west through the Golden Triangle of tourism in northern India, which includes Rajasthan and the Pink City of Jaipur.

The Dusty Land

Rajasthan, legendary land of camels, dust and commerce. Hot and dry as a furnace with brickworks piled up along the highway and not much else in between the thorn trees and the sand.

"See any moose out there?" Jeannette asks as we bump across a desert plain on a bus.

"Ha-ha, herds of them."

A huge 20-wheel dump truck rattles past us, crammed with riders. All of the faces of India are onboard, from babies and toddlers to grandmas and old men in their bright linens and turbans, their faces cracked wide in smiles as they see us and wave. A family of eight is hanging off the tailgate of the truck alongside a bamboo ladder while a dozen or so riders perch on top in the full sun. Dozens of bags dangle over the edge of the truck. Some toddlers and their mammas gaze somberly from two small portals at the side of the truck as we pass by.

"That must be the local bus," Jeannette says. "There must be 30 people onboard."

"It doesn't look very safe," I note, "but it does look like a lot of fun."

Jaipur is a lively town, home to an ancient observatory full of sweeping curves and sight lines that had the Indians of long ago tracking the moon, planets and stars for their astrological divinations.

Bird-like women flutter in the marketplace, as thin as wrens and tiny as children, their faces hidden behind the veils of their saris - orange, purple, red and blue - hoping in their shy way to remain invisible from roaming eyes.

We join a line of tourists hiking far up a sloping path to the Amber

Fort past a long line of beggars of every variety; people who are missing arms, legs, feet and hands, with the tangle-haired insane among
them, crusted in dirt and huddled against a wall, some having limbs
twisted in agonizing angles. A dark man with searching eyes and a
high turban pulls a large black cobra from a basket, one of many people doing photo ops here as a business venture.

"Think of all the millions of people who must have worked on this
place," Jeannette says as we reach the top of a tower overlooking miles
of countryside. "Think of the elephants that pulled all these stones up
here."

"Think of all the thousands of forts and palaces and pyramids around
the world and all the millions who worked on them," I say. "Some
people like to imagine that they're reincarnations of kings or queens,
but most of our ancestors were probably slaves at one time or another."

"Maybe we even worked on this place in a past life."

"Maybe, but it doesn't look all that familiar."

A Night at the Palace

One of the perks of being a tourist in India is that for the price of a
budget motel back home you can spend the night in a palace, many
of which have been converted into hotels by maharajahs who can no
longer afford their upkeep.

Jeannette and I spend the night in a 400-year-old palace at Roopangarh Fort outside a periwinkle blue village of the same name. The
town is also distinguished by the large number of hairy hogs wandering its streets.

The boars lap mop-gray sewage from the open drains around town,
bumbling along between mobs of children, scrawny dogs, goats and
cows. These pigs have personality, wild, spiky-punk hair-dos, open
sores, and they're dirtier than any pig across the sea could imagine. Who eats them? Not Hindus, only tribal people living out in the
scrubs.

We are pleased to see that the iron-clad gate of the fort is angled so that
no war elephant can get a running start to batter it down while we're
sleeping; plus there are 8-inch spikes in the door as a further deterrent,
and many rusty old swords on the wall should I need one. Camels

graze in the courtyard and peacocks flutter on the castle walls.

We stay in what was the maharajah's bedroom, which is nearly half the size of our entire home back in Michigan. The colossal bed has a carved headboard of lacquered ebony that rises to the ceiling, beautifully painted with red flowers; and although there are no concubines to frolic with, I get a chance to play maharajah for the day.

It's possible that Sting snoozed in the same room, as photos on the wall show that the rock star was also a guest here.

That evening for a small fee, the villagers dress us in the traditional garb of a maharani queen and a maharajah to dine by candlelight in the courtyard under the stars. It's a local business, dressing tourists like this, and it would be cruel to decline. I feel silly in my poofy red turban, but Jeannette looks a perfect princess in her sari of burgundy and gold. Dinner is a delicious tandoori chicken marinated in salt, yogurt and spices.

Even the poorest Western backpacker in India is a millionaire compared to the average Indian citizen, who might slave all day in the 90-degree sun for the equivalent of a dollar or two. Back in Jaipur, a cab driver told us that he drives a 12-hour shift, six days a week.

Although the people of India may be poor and overworked, they dress extremely well in Sunday-best clothes, whereas most of us backpackers are slobs in tank tops and flip flops.

Good grooming is extremely important here as a way to set individuals apart from the squalor of their surroundings. Men are said to account for 40 percent of the beauty shop visits in India, and even if a razor-thin young man has nothing more than a handful of rupees to his name, he dresses as flashy as if he is on top of the world.

It's also said that the typical woman in India owns 200 saris, which are 18-foot lengths of fabric ranging from $10 to $10,000 for a fancy wedding outfit.

So it's rather odd to be waited on by six sharp-dressed men who hover over your every move while you're dressed like Beavis and Butthead. Although I begrudge taking up extra room in our backpacks, we've purchased some dressy clothes so that we can show respect to the locals by sprucing up at dinner time.

Playing dress-up as royalty to support the locals is a bit of mandatory fun, but we don't kid ourselves that it's all smiles and good vibes for tourists in India. Beneath the poverty we find veins of resentment. While walking through Roopangarh the next day, an elderly man gives out a hearty "Bah!" of contempt when we say hello and a woman denounces us: "You are lazy people who do nothing, while we are the hard-working people," she says.

She's got a point.

Resentment doomed many a maharajah. Getting murdered by your sons, tossed down a well, poisoned, or pricked by daggers in the night were occupational hazards.

So we're happy to surrender our throne the next day, heading west for the sacred city of Pushkar.

Johnny the Camel

A beater jeep, bare as as skillet, runs us along a single-track pathway in the desert through tribal villages where some people still live in tents bleached by the sun. We roll past rough fields of upturned clods baked hard as clay in the eternal sun. What grows here? Beans, legumes and dry crops. We're well into the high summer's heat and the rains of June are yet to come.

Pushkar is the holy city of Brahma, god of creation. It's also the site of a world-famous camel fair each November that brings in 50,000 camels and a similar number of tourists. Where they stack them all we can't imagine.

With that many camels, a desert campout is on the "must-do" list of activities for those visiting Pushkar. We lope on a line of camels through town, feeling as grand as caravan raiders but drawing no interest from the locals - we're just another knot of overindulged tourists out on camel safari. Several miles out of town, we camp beneath a cathedral of southern stars.

Dust, dust, dust, swirling at your feet, dyeing your heels black, filling your nostrils, invading your ears, burning your eyes. The grit of powdered camel shit in your teeth, down your pants, in your nose; dust here and there, dust everywhere. Our campground is a field of camel shit dust.

My camel stands about seven-feet-tall and is named Johnny. A camel is a bony beast and Johnny has a beaded saddle. By the second day of bouncing up and down in the desert, Johnny has tenderized my rear-end like a piece of raw meat, a parting gift from India as we head west to the Arab lands.

"No, I don't mind walking," I wave off the camel tenders on the way back to town when my saddle slips off and slides upside down under Johnny's tummy. "Not a problem."

Other than its camels, Pushkar is a shopping Nirvana. Amid its hundreds of shops we have reached the highest plane of tourist reincarnation. Stalls line a narrow street through town and, as if by a miracle, there is no hassle nor need to bargain - the prices are fixed. Jeannette buys little girl dresses for the grandkids back home along with jackets to prepare for the chills of Turkey.

"These are made of camel wool," the tailor says of our jackets, meaning old cut-up blankets of the sort we sleep under at night; heavy, thick wool as warm as Christmas. Our glorified sweatshirts have towering hoods that make us look like Smurfs.

Young, European backpackers wander around Pushkar dressed as Hindu gods or like the villagers of Kipling's time, bare-chested with beads, tattoos and kohl eyes. Ironically, no proper Indian would dream of dressing this way today, except perhaps on a temple pilgrimage as a lark. Indian men all look like they've stepped out of the pages of a J.C. Penney catalogue with dress pants, sport shirts and loafers.

Hmmm... rice and lentils, lentils and rice. Curried potatoes, cauliflower and okra with saffron lentils and more rice. What's for lunch? Lentils and rice, perhaps. What's for dinner? Rice and lentils, most likely.

No meat is served in a holy city, not even an egg. And no beer. Getting caught with a beer in Pushkar or the sacred areas of Varanasi and Hampi can get you arrested, possibly even thrown in jail. We smuggle a liter of Kingfisher beer into town and drink it warm in our room, wrestling with what to do with the empty bottle. It ends up under our bed.

One last train hauls us back to the hubbub of Delhi where we say farewell to new friends and old India, perhaps never to return.

The Dubie Brothers

With our eyes as wide as saucers, we speed through the darkness after midnight in a cab through the fabulous city of Dubai. We see vague shapes of architectural wonders in the darkness and mile after mile of new hotels, restaurants and shopping malls.

"Quite a switch from India, isn't it?" Jeannette says.

"Yeah, this is like a decompression chamber to get us back into the real world," I say.

"I wouldn't call this the real world by a long shot," she says.

We arrive in Dubai on April 1 via Air India in a plane full of surly Indian businessmen. Some fool was transporting a crate of live cobras that got out and slithered all over the cabin. Quite an uproar as you can imagine.

I have some deep apprehensions about going to Dubai because a year or so ago I had mailed a copy of my first book, "Planet Backpacker," to a friend living here and never heard if she received it. The book had some unkind things to say about the state of Islam today, and since I knew that censors are said to go through the mail in Dubai, I had talked myself into a state of paranoia over the possibility of being on some sort of watch list. Would I be arrested at the airport? Beheaded in the public square? After all, the Saudis had sent a plane all the way to Malaysia to seize a journalist who merely tweeted about Muhammad.

But there are perhaps 1,000 tourists waiting to get through customs at the airport and clearly the Dubies have more on their minds than messing with little old mixed-up me.

Before you could say jumping genies, we are in the hotel bar, puffing on the apple-flavored tobacco of a hookah. And after staying at the scroungiest sort of places in Asia, our digs in Dubai are over the moon. I had reserved the cheapest room in a modest hotel near the marina district and this turned out to be a full suite with a kitchen, washing machine, dryer, living room and computerized TV.

"Oh, the rugged backpacking life," I say as we recline on a bed fit for a sheik.

"I feel like a princess," Jeannette says.

"Well, you are a hobo princess after all. I read it in your blog."

"Whatever, this is a nice change from India. On our last day there, all the noise and the crowds and the dirt started getting to me."

"But we survived."

"Oh yeah," Jeannette says, taking another puff on the water pipe.

Dubai is a city-state in the United Arab Emirates. The UAE is a hodge-podge of seven sandy kingdoms oozing with oil wealth on the Arabian Peninsula. The kingdoms banded together for their mutual protection in 1971.

A linear city that runs for 18 miles along the Persian Gulf, Dubai is the wealthiest city in the Mideast and the Land of Shopping. Thousands of people fly in each week from all over the world to shop at its malls and some of the most expensive stores in the world.

There's something of a disconnect in the UAE, however, in that some of its super rich denizens provided funding for Al Qaeda and possibly even the disaster of 9/11. Wouldn't these foes of modernity just love to cut down the blaspheming Westerners who crowd their shopping malls?

But that is painting with a broad brush, as there seem to be plenty of Dubie brothers who have a live-and-let-live outlook, and indeed, secretly wish they could cut loose and party like their Western visitors.

As in Singapore, KL and Sydney, we walk ourselves silly, trying to take it all in. We see the indoor ski hill at a mall where Arab kids don snow suits and snowboard past animatronic polar bears and penguins. We check out another mall's walk-through aquarium. Then there's the ice skating rink and spectacular water fountain show next to what is now the world's tallest building. We check out the spice bazaar and gold souk in town, but a chorus of harassment to buy copy watches and handbags soon drives us away.

"Muslim shop owners never seem to have a clue that if they'd just shut up and let you look they'd have 10 times as many sales," I grumble.

"How many watches can anyone own, anyway?" Jeannette says.

Good question, because beyond the copy watches in the souk, there are dozens of stores in the malls selling real luxury watches for tens of thousands of dollars. Who buys them all?

That's about all anyone needs to know about Dubai, except that it has a very nice monorail system which runs much of the way along its coast.

You'd think with all its wealth that Dubai would be a wonderland for its citizens. Yet the dark brown men of Dubai on the metro train are among the glummest bunch of dead-eyed drones I've ever seen, and I can't imagine they make much more than slave wages.

They remind me of the similarly gloom-stricken French commuters bound for the dismal suburbs of Paris. Yet who can blame them? Men of the Arabian Peninsula are barely allowed to even talk to women, much less date them, and at any rate, many Arab women dress like Darth Vader in acres of black chador. It's a Man's World here, and it sucks.

But Dubai is just a lily pad on our hop-skip east to Turkey.

The Deep Freeze

We get a chilly reception in transit. We arrive at the airport in Bahrain near midnight with the expectation of being put up in town by our carrier, Gulf Air, since it's an overnight stopover on the way to Turkey. This gets the thumbs-down from a counter attendant and it turns out that visas would be $80 for the two or us, with a hotel the same for a stay of a few hours.

So we're stuck in the airport overnight in its freezing air conditioning until our plane to Istanbul leaves at 9 a.m.

"It feels cold enough to snow in here," Jeannette says as we huddle to keep warm.

"Let's hope we don't get frostbite," I say through chattering teeth.

With all of our extra clothing tucked away in the baggage for tomorrow's plane, there's nothing we can do but shiver. Unable to sleep, we shake through the night in our light clothing while it's in the 80s just a few inches away outside the windows of the terminal. Of course, we can't venture outside without passing customs and then the hassle of returning through immigration and the security rigamarole of entering an airport, so we're stuck in the 'fridge.

Fortunately, Jeannette has a silk shawl to cuddle up with. My angel also finds an Arabic newspaper for me which serves as a hobo blanket.

Perhaps our Arctic conditions are an improvement over staying in town since Bahrain is undergoing that curious modern condition where a civil war is simmering while life goes on without a beat. The island kingdom is ruled by a minority of wealthy Sunnis, lording it over an impoverished population of Shiites who make up 70 percent of Bahrain's 650,000 citizens. The fighting in the streets has died to a lull, but rears its head periodically as one of the uprisings of the Arab Spring.

Talking Turkey

"Ask any world traveler what their favorite place is and chances are they'll say Turkey," I say as we haul our packs off a sleek light rail train in the heart of Istanbul.

"I'm loving it," Jeannette says. With a big gray pack on her back and a front pack clutched to her chest, my beaming wife looks the part of an adventurer in the cosmopolitan center of what was once known as Constantinople. Atop her head is the straw hat we bought back in Airlie Beach, Australia.

"I'm proud of you," I say.

"Why? We're doing the same thing."

"Yeah, but who else would be marching around Istanbul with a backpack and a long, flowing skirt at our age?"

Istanbul is the link between Europe and Asia and a great crossroads of the world. Currently, the city is being trumpeted in scores of travel publications and websites as a must-visit destination. Thousands of tourists mill through its squares, with many from East Europe and Central Asia. With a babel of languages ringing in our ears, it's impossible to tell who's a Turk and who's from Russia, Greece, Ukraine, Georgia, the Baltic, Macedonia, Albania, Kazakhstan...

Modern Turkey, like Communist China, Cuba and the old Soviet Union, is a product of radical social engineering. At the end of World War I with the Ottoman Empire was falling apart, a Turkish army officer named Mustafa Kemal Ataturk led a revolution known as the

Turkish War of Independence. The George Washington of his country, Ataturk defeated the Western allies sent to crush his revolt. He established the Republic of Turkey.

But more than that, he established a secular, democratic government which gave women equal rights and created a free public education system, ridding Turkey of the meddling of Muslim clerics and religious fanatics. Turkey has since become the model dream state of the Arab Spring movement.

Istanbul offers a checklist of sights dating from pre-Medieval times, starting with the Blue Mosque and the huge dome of the Hagia Sophia, which was the cathedral of the Eastern Holy Roman Empire. We get lost in the Grand Bazaar, the oldest and largest shopping center on earth with 3,000 shops ranging along 61 covered lanes. A dozen or so mosques perch atop the hills of the city, sparkling like crowns topped by the needle spires of their minarets - "Bright and clean" in the sun, to quote Ernest Hemingway, who passed through here as a war correspondent at the age of 23.

Hemingway was one of many writers who lingered in Istanbul, including Graham Greene, Agatha Christie and Lord Byron, who famously swam the Bosphorous, a strait that connects the Black Sea to the Mediterranean.

It's not all old-timey stuff in Istanbul, however. In the "new" part of town a broad thoroughfare is packed with what seems like 100,000 people ranging up and down for a mile or so with the side streets brimming with cafes and jazz clubs. The action here goes on until sunrise.

The Circuit

A ferry takes us across the tiny Sea of Marmara and we push on by bus on a circuit which will take us around western Turkey. As is the case with India's Golden Triangle of tourism, there's a loop around this half of the country that takes in Turkey's greatest hits.

Today is Easter Sunday, and the best celebration I can think of is to be sitting on a bus on a spring day in Turkey with brave and beautiful Jeannette.

We glide through green, rolling hills dotted with farms, villages and grazing sheep. A heart-lifting river valley looks as lush as Ireland,

and in the distance are snow-capped mountains. Tulips, daffodils and flowering trees line the road and groves of olive trees pass by our window as we roll into the city of Bursa.

Bursa was once the eastern terminus of the Silk Road, which wandered for thousands of miles to India and China.

"Imagine the excitement people felt, leaving here a thousand years ago to cross all of Asia in a camel caravan," I say.

"I bet they were even happier to get back, if they made it," Jeannette says. "They must have been gone for years."

"Well, we made it."

"Not by camel, though, and not down the dusty old Silk Road."

"I think I would have walked the whole way, come to think of it," I say, reflecting on our bumpy camel ride in India.

Bursa is also where the country of Turkey was born in 1326 when a sultan named Orhan laid siege to the city. Orhan was leader of the Ottoman Turks, who sprang from Central Asia. At the time, Bursa was held by the Byzantines, who were the Christians of the Holy Roman Empire.

The Turks surrounded Bursa for 10 years and starved the Byzantines into submission, ending their 1,000-year empire. The newcomers gave the Anatolian Peninsula a new name: Land of the Turks.

Things have calmed down considerably since then. At an open air shopping mall in the heart of Bursa we see excited women digging through pyramids of bras, underwear and blouses as if excavating ancient Turkey itself.

Bible Study

The tourist trail inevitably leads to Ephesus, the 3,000-year-old ruins of the best-preserved city of the classical world.

Ephesus played a role in the wrap-up of the New Testament, for it was here that the apostle Paul lived from 52-54 A.D., preaching against the worship of Artemis (aka Diana), the patron goddess of the city during Roman rule.

Artemis was a fertility goddess who is often depicted with dozens of breasts; she looks a bit like a pine cone with all those boobs. Paul got into a spot of trouble with the local artisans, who sold statues of the goddess; he was imprisoned in a tower for being a nuisance. He wrote the Corinthians chapter of the Bible here, and later, the Letter to the Ephesians.

It's also possible that the apostle John wrote the Book of Revelations in Ephesus, having heard his weird tale of the end of the world directly from God Himself through a hole in the wall of a cave on the nearby island of Patmos. Ephesus is also said to have been the final home of Mary, the mother of Jesus.

"What I like about Ephesus most is all of the cats," Jeannette says as we snap yet another photo of a kitty lounging by the ancient baths, the old brothel, the amphitheater and the skeleton of the city's library. "It's like each site in the city has its own cat, ready for a photo-op."

Only cats live here now, but once upon a time, Ephesus had a population of more than 50,000 and was one of the most important ports on the Mediterranean. Through the years, its harbor silted up and turned to marsh. Eventually, the city was stranded miles from the sea. Deprived of its reason for existence, it fell into ruin.

Smacked Around

I'm not used to getting a hearty smack on the ass from another man, but this is a signal that my soapy massage is almost done.

This is the "end result" of our visit to a traditional Turkish bath in Selcuk, which proves to be about as relaxing as Jeannette and I can handle.

Dressed only in towels, we are led into a large steam room, the center of which is a circular marble slab about 13 feet in diameter. You lie baking and sweating on the table for up to an hour until you're quite light-headed. Then it's over to another marble bench where a hefty gent works you over with a felt mitten, scrubbing your body from head to toe.

By felt mitten, I mean a virtual Brillo pad that feels like it's ripping the skin right off my chest. There goes months of tan - patches on my back and chest are scrubbed raw.

Then, the soapy massage from head to toe, a shampoo and a cold shower. This is all followed up by an oil massage provided by a burly man with thumbs of steel. He squeezes the muscles of your calves like toothpaste through a tube and digs what must be the point of his elbow into your back and chest in such a steely concentration of pain that you wonder if he's going to crack your ribs.

Wonderful sensation, although it makes me realize that there's a thin line between a giggle and a scream.

"There's a momentum to travel, isn't there?" I say as we head south. "It feels like we're charging around the world, going faster and faster."

"We sure are," Jeannette says. "Every country seems more intense than the one we just left. You cross a border and everything changes."

"It's like each new place is another crescendo or a wave."

"Planet waves," she says, gazing out the window of our train as the farmlands of Turkey roll by.

"I sure don't want to go home, I'm loving this," she says at last.

"You know, if we wanted to, we could sell everything we own and just keep traveling for the rest of our lives," I say.

"Wouldn't we run out of money?"

"Not if we sold our house. That would keep us traveling for at least 20 years. We could live in different countries for a few months or years and then move on."

"It would get old, and I don't think I could eat rice and beans for the rest of my life," Jeannette says. "And what would we do when we finally went broke?"

"Pick fruit for a living, maybe. Or we could just call it quits and jump off a cliff. We'd be in our 80s by then."

"That's not much of an option. Plus, we've got a lot of things to do back home, and I want to see the baby."

Back home, daughter Chloe has delivered a baby boy, her first. We didn't learn of her pregnancy until we were on the verge of leaving on our trip and Jeannette has felt a mixture of guilt and longing ever since for not being at Chloe's side at the birth. But it was too late to change our plans and too expensive to fly home from the far side of the world. In any event, Jeannette would have missed the birth because baby Zach has arrived a month early.

Jeannette's father is also deathly ill in Florida, all while Nathan and the four grandkids are struggling with the trials of a broken family in our home. Family is the come-along tugging us home and I feel the gravity of a hairball the size of Jupiter pulling us in that direction.

A sense of familial duty dampens my fantasy of traveling on forever.

That, and we're almost broke. Four year's of savings have gone squirreled away into the pockets of merchants, taxi drivers, air lines, hostels and hotels around the world. And ahead lies the sybaritic expense of Italy.

"I don't think I could handle using grotty public toilets and riding on crowded buses for the rest of my life, come to think of it," I say, leaving out the part about us going bust.

But nasty toilets and bumpy rides aside, there's a part of both of us that would like to just keep going.

Rolling hills covered with thousands of olive trees pass by the window of our sleek new train as we push on. Far below, I catch sight of three donkeys frolicking in a pasture by a river. Turkey is a fertile land, and it's easy to see why it was coveted by so many tribes and nations in the Bible.

The armies of Alexander the Great, Rome, Persia, Greece, Britain, Egypt, France, Genghis Khan, Russia, the Huns, the Crusades, the Ottoman Empire and even Australia and New Zealand all had their day here, making a mess of the place.

But these old haunts of the Hittites, the Philistines and the tribes of Abraham are now covered with a network of new roads, towns and shopping centers, all mixed amid a jumble of ramshackle huts and villages that conjure up the 1800s.

In the town of Selcuk, the ruins of an ancient aqueduct run through the business district, topped by nesting storks. It's a curious mix of the modern and the old. As is said, Turkey is one big open-air museum.

Land of the Gods

Our bus winds along a coastal road on the Mediterranean coast beneath Mount Olympus. Unfortunately, we fail to catch a glimpse of the home of the gods because Big MO is shrouded in clouds.

Rats!

"I thought Mt. Olympus was in Greece," I say, craning for a view. "I read all the myths of Zeus and the gods when I was a kid, but always thought that Mt. Olympus was a fictional place like Asgard."

Somewhere up there, the gods are in their gleaming temples, sitting down to lunch with plates of gold filled with soul food. The adventures of Perseus, Hercules, Orpheus, Apollo, Athena, Neptune and such always got back to the dinner table in the old myths where the gossipy gods mulled over the affairs of men and immortals, lending a hand here and there.

"Yet here it is, hidden in the fog," I mutter.

But Jeannette doesn't have time for the gods; she's busy communicating with a young deaf Turkish woman, typing back and forth on our iPad. Although she can't hear, she has managed to learn English in school and seems thrilled by Jeannette's attention.

Long before the birth of Christ, portions of coastal Turkey were part of the Greek empire which stretched all the way to Italy, Sicily and Spain. Back when Zeus was casting thunderbolts, Mt. Olympus was part of the Grecian world.

It's a sacred mountain in that it is home to the chimera, or eternal flame. Far up its slopes are volcanic vents which glow flame-red in the night. I'd love to climb its slope and spend the night with Venus Aphrodite, watching the sun rise with the old gods, but the hike will have to wait until another lifetime.

One of the hazards of traveling in Europe is that sooner or later you run into someone who really stinks. Such is our fate when a man gets on the bus who smells like he hasn't bathed in weeks, if ever. Naturally, he sits next to me and we are squished four-across at the rear of the bus. He smells so bad that he stinks up the whole bus.

Among the Ghosts

Moving on, we spend a night in the Ghost Village of Kayakoy.

We wander through the ruins of hundreds of skeletal brick houses, businesses and Greek Orthodox churches. Nothing is left but thin frames of stone.

"It looks like an atom bomb fell on this place," Jeannette says as we climb to a chapel high above the village. "But it's all just the work of Mother Nature."

"All in less than 100 years."

Kayakoy is where 3,000 citizens of Greek descent were forced to leave the country in 1924. Following Turkey's War of Independence in 1922-23 there was a swap of citizens in which all of the Greeks in

Turkey and all of the Turks in Greece were forced to leave their homes and return to their native lands.

This was a ethnic cleansing tragedy of immense suffering, since the newcomers often didn't even know the language of their long-ago homelands and in any case, weren't welcome. Today, the United States does much the same thing, sending the children of illegal immigrants back to Mexico, even those who've spent their entire lives in the U.S. and don't speak Spanish.

The ruins of Kayakoy are a contrast to the serenity of the Blue Water Coast along a sea of sapphire blue which is literally over the next hill. The coast is the haunt of the ancient Lycians and villages that have basked in the sun for 4,000 years.

This playground along the southwestern shores of Turkey is packed with tens of thousands of tourists, with the big draw being a Blue Water cruise of several days aboard a fleet of wooden yachts. Alas, it's an overcast, gray water day when we arrive, producing more shivers than sunshine.

Land of the Muslims

"How should a bird fly except with its own kind?"

- Rumi

It's a bit spooky walking around the city of Konya at night, not because this is one of the most conservative Muslim cities on the Anatolian plain, but because our guide, Cucu (pronounced Ju-Ju), is nervous about stopping here.

"People here don't like people like me," he says. "They know where I'm from and they don't like us."

Apparently, the Turks of Konya can tell that Cucu is an outsider by his accent, just as an American can discern the accent of a Southerner or a native New Yorker in an instant.

But our little band of backpackers has a pleasant stroll through the busy streets of the city late in the evening. If there are any jihadists here, perhaps they're all off blogging somewhere when we pass through. The gangs of young men we see clowning around are all college students, some on their way to tea rooms where acoustic music is being played for entertainment.

"Isn't it nice that the young people here have lives that don't revolve around drinking?" says John, a backpacker in his 70s from Australia. "In Australia all the young people are always in the bars or getting drunk at parties."

Watching the young Muslim students laughing and having fun over tiny glasses of apple tea, I have to admit that there's a healthful side to Islam that's lacking in the West.

Konya is the home of Mawlana Rumi, the poet and philosopher who was born to a family of theologians in 1207. He and his family fled to this town to escape an invasion of the Mongol horde.

Rumi was introduced to the mystical path by a wandering dervish holy man. He created the Sufi order, a brotherhood that offers a gentler form of Islam, celebrating Allah through music, dance and lyrical poetry.

One way this sect connects with Allah is through the Whirling Dervishes. These are men dressed in circus colors and parachute pants who spin like tops for an hour or so, attaining a state of spiritual ecstasy for the entertainment of packed houses.

We visit Rumi's mosque, where we gaze on 1,000-year-old texts inscribed in golden letters by hand in exquisite penmanship on books of faded linen. In the gift shop, I buy a book of Rumi's sayings, exhorting readers to take up the spiritual life; but most of his words have grown impossibly antique and obscure in the 700 years since the poet's death. Yet here is one that might apply to travelers: "A little river which is moving constantly does not become polluted or grow fetid."

High in Cappadocia

We veer north for one of the wonders of the travel world: Cappadocia.

Rush hour in Cappadocia in central Turkey means a sky crowded with 70 hot air balloons that fly more than 300 days a year. Hundreds of people cram a departure hall, scarfing a rudimentary breakfast from Styrofoam cups and plates before liftoff at sunrise.

We see a horde of excited Asian tourists pouring into huge gondolas that carry up to 24 passengers.

"Crapazoids, that looks scary!" Jeannette says as we float up like a soap bubble with a modest group of six. "I wouldn't want to be in a balloon with that many people."

"It would sure go down with a sickening splat," I agree.

Below are twisting canyons and hundreds of fairy castles. These are rock outcroppings shaped like 100-foot-tall sweet potatoes which are honeycombed with caves. Some of the caves date back 4,000 years and serve as hotels, shops and homes.

This is one of Turkey's premier tourist destinations. The weird hobbit homes, fairy chimneys and limestone puddings are unlike anything on earth.

I'm more fearful of the expense than the threat of falling out of our balloon; it's a dizzying $150 each for an hour or so aloft.

"Every balloon pilot in the world wants to fly here," our Australian pilot assures us. "I've flown around the world from New Mexico to Africa and the Outback, but Cappadocia is the clincher."

After our ride we wander for miles through the canyon lands, a place as otherworldly as anything you'd see in a Star Wars film. Our hike takes us through Love Valley, which has hundreds of penis-shaped rocks, many over 100 feet tall and quite erect.

"Very inspiring for the ladies, I imagine."

"Well, it does give you something to think about," Jeannette says.

Near the town of Gerome are dozens of underground cities, some of which ramble more than 200 feet below the surface. At one time, these subterranean cities hid the ancient Hittites from invaders, and then the early Christians from Roman soldiers.

We visit one of the best-known hideouts, discovered only a few decades ago. It's a creepy crawl, wriggling our way down a crazy-quilt network of low, narrow tunnels 120 feet underground.

"People must have been a lot skinnier back then," Jeannette says as we squeeze like toothpaste through a sandstone portal.

"I imagine some fat tourists get stuck down here now and then," I answer, shuddering at the thought.

Here, far underground, up to 1,000 people could hide for months, with special rooms for their food, wine and chapels. An air shaft plunges into blackness deep into the earth, well below where we're allowed to visit. It's estimated that more than 60 of these underground refuges are scattered around the countryside, many still undiscovered.

Later, our group of backpackers sits on pillows at a hookah bar back in Cappadocia, puffing at our pipes and drinking pints of beer with travelers from all over the Earth.

Tears fill Cucu's eyes as we talk about where we're moving on to.

"I'm not doing this anymore. This is my last trip," he says.

"What's wrong?"

"I get to be such good friends with people from all over the world, but only for two weeks and then they're gone and I never see them again," he says, his face streaming wet. "I can't take it anymore."

The Poor Man's Italy

Our Croatian Airlines propeller plane is 45 minutes late getting off the runway in Istanbul, so we don't arrive in Zagreb, the capital of Croatia, until 11 p.m.

"Another night of landing in a strange place with an unknown language and only a vague idea of where to go," I fret. The roads outside the airport are empty and there aren't any taxis roaming around. If we get lost we'll have to bivouac on the streets.

But as if by magic a bus shows up, and after wandering around some darkened streets for a bit, we manage to find our well-hidden hotel. Once again, Fortune smiles on some traveling fools.

Known as the "poor man's Italy," Croatia is all the rage with travel writers, owing to its medieval villages, Roman ruins, pebbled beaches and outdoor café scene. The women are said to be among the most beautiful in Europe, the wine flows like water, and there are ancient ruins to explore around every corner.

Croatia also offers some of the best sailing in Europe along the necklace of islands off its coast. This country along the Adriatic Sea brims with tourists from neighboring Slovenia, Italy and Germany who pour across the border in search of travel bargains.

"Bargain" is a relative term, however. We have a pleasant day wandering around the markets and sidewalk cafés of Zagreb's Old Town and then take a bus from the capital 100 miles to the seaside resort of Opatija, passing through miles of forested hill country, followed by gorgeous views of the Adriatic Sea.

With no hotel reservations, we're dismayed to find that Opatija is packed with expensive Italianate hotels by the sea which all look to be in the $200-per-night range or more. We trudge up and down the main drag with our packs under a cloud of dismal choices.

But we see signs for "Apartman" which I take to be pensiones, the European term for "guest room," and soon enough a local hails us with an invite to stay at his place for 50 euros. Jeannette talks him down to 40 (about $60 U.S.) and we land in a fine place with a kitchen overlooking the sea. Again, backpackers luck.

Setting Sail

The thing to do in old Croatia these days is to cruise and cycle the islands of the Dalmatian coast via an armada of pleasure boats.

This all depends on the season. It's far too hot to cycle the islands in the high summer, so boat operators offer bicycle tours only in the spring and fall, sandwiched around the more lucrative cruising season.

This being spring, we board the "Dalmanika" the next day, a wooden yacht with two masts which will be our home for a week on the islands south of the Istrian Peninsula. Our shipmates include six Slovenians, some Germans, Austrians, two Danish girls and a British couple. They seem surprised that two Americans are onboard. It's not like we're zebras, but apparently we're unexpected in this corner of the world.

Despite all of the gush about Croatia in the travel publications, by one estimate only 15,000 Americans make it here each year out of more than 10 million annual tourists, and I imagine most of the Yanks are cruise ship visitors to Split and Dubrovnik.

"Just nod and smile," I say as we try communicating with a red-faced but robust German in his 60s who turns out to be the best cyclist among us. "For all I know, he's asking if you're wearing any underpants."

"For the first time on our trip, we can't communicate with half of the people we're with," Jeannette says, smiling and nodding on cue.

This is because English is the linguistic currency of most of the world today, or at least any place interested in getting ahead. We've had no trouble speaking with locals in Indonesia, Thailand, India, Sri Lanka,

Malaysia and Turkey. But middle-aged German cyclists? *Nicht*.

As promised, the hilly islands of Croatia are a thigh-burning challenge. Bonus: also very windy and cold at times in mid-April. Our first ride is only 9 miles, but gives notice to how out of shape our cycling legs are. We suck!

"Thank God we bought those track suits!" Jeannette says on our ride through a downpour the next day, swaddled in her flapping poncho over the outfits we bought "just in case" at the last minute in Istanbul's Grand Bazaar. "We'd have hypothermia without them."

"Congrats, you look like a licorice jelly bean again with that poncho flapping around."

"A jelly bean on a bike."

Indeed. We cycle 25 miles in a cold rain, but have a hilarious time nonetheless, stopping by a winery for a lunch of bread, sheep cheese and prosciutto. Also, three glasses of wine and two of schnapps. Our German, Austrian and Slovenian comrades like their drink, and soon everyone is laughing and having a great time at a rustic winery in the hills. Later, some of the older Germans toss off their clothes and leap naked into the Adriatic after a chilly ride in the wind.

"Do you ever stop smiling?" I ask as we roll into the port of Rab.

"It doesn't get any better than this," Jeannette says, soggy as a sponge and beaming from ear to ear.

"I don't think you've stopped smiling once on this whole trip."

"That's just what I do."

"You're always kind of a wimp when it comes to biking in the rain back home," I note.

"Yeah, but this is different. I don't have any choice, so I may as well enjoy it."

The Echo of Guns

Last week was the 20th anniversary of the Bosnian War in this part of the world, but no one was celebrating. More than 100,000 people died here in the early '90s and 2.2 million were displaced by ethnic cleansing. The intentional murder of civilians by snipers and artillery, the systematic rape of up to 50,000 women, mass graves and the genocide of Muslim civilians were hallmarks of the Bosnian War.

The war was the result of the breakup of the Yugoslavian Federation after the fall of communism. Yugoslavia was made up of eight countries and districts, filled with ethnically-diverse people who hated each others' guts.

It was the same story as in Iraq: when the communist dictatorship of Yugoslavia fell, the Croatian Catholics, Muslim Bosniaks and Orthodox Serbs were unleashed to settle old grudges, driving the weak from their homes, often into mass graves.

"I used to hear the sound of the bombs and the cannon on the mainland when I was growing up," says our cycle leader, Boyan. He was raised on the island of Rab where we are stranded for a day by heavy seas. "I was too young to join the army then. Maybe I wouldn't be here today if I was older, yes?"

Bosnia, in the heart of Yugoslavia, never recovered. Bosnia suffers from long-term poverty and a youth unemployment rate of 57 percent. This is the price of war – something for us to think about in America, which always seems to be headed down that road.

The Golden Fleece

Our fourth day of cycling dawns sunny and clear as crystal. We roll past 400-year-old olive trees and miles of rock walls piled waist-high by peasant farmers over hundreds of years. A lamb and her mama stop in front of me in the road, their wool backlit a flaming gold in the morning sun. Have we stumbled on the Golden Fleece, the fabled treasure of Jason and the Argonauts? Maybe not, but we have found the sunny side of spring in Croatia.

"Have you noticed there's a different meaning to the word 'flat' in Croatia?" Jeannette says as we labor up another long hill. "'Flat' in Croatia means a long, slow ride uphill for an hour or so."

"If this is flat then what do they consider a hill?"

"Straight up. I think their idea of a hill is our idea of a mountain."

But the hills just make the end of each ride all the sweeter. We dine each night at outdoor cafés in a different port, doing our best to decrease Croatia's store of wine. The poor man's Italy, found!

It's fruitless to describe the scenery here: you just have to go and see for yourself. Twenty of us roll past miles of stony hills and olive groves on our mountain bikes. We climb a road hundreds of feet above the sea, with views of distant islands and mountains. Flocks of sheep "baa" by the side of the road, often rushing across it in a river of wool. We roll on for 20-30 miles through villages with stone towers overlooking squares filled with outdoor cafes. Then past ruined chapels that have stood watch by the sea for 1,500 years.

Later, I strum my guitar on deck as the islands float by. All too soon, the song is over.

To Tuscany

Seven months ago, Jeannette and I were undecided as to where to end our trip. Rome won the toss with Paris, and now we are sadly on the home stretch, heading for Italy.

Two fellow cyclists give us a ride in their car through tiny Slovenia to Trieste. Milanis is a Slovene contractor who speaks good English, asking me many questions about life in America.

"There are a lot of good things about America, but on the other hand, you have universal health care for everyone who lives in Slovenia and we don't," I say, reflecting on the absurdity that a country the size of Delaware can accomplish something that confounds the U.S. Congress.

"Maybe that's because you spend all your money on the military," Milanis offers.

"Yeah, I think so."

Bidding our goodbyes, we hike around in the broiling sun for two miles or so, sweating buckets before finding a small hotel in the heart of the old town.

Located on the border of northeastern Italy, Trieste is where James Joyce wrote his epic "Ulysses," about a day in the life of Dublin. Apparently, Joyce was persona non grata in Ireland for his gritty take on *The Dubliners*. He fled to Trieste to cook up an even saltier take on his home turf with *Ulysses*. Now, of course, he's practically lauded as a saint in Ireland and there's a bronze statue of him in the heart of Trieste.

This city is also where adventurer Sir Richard Burton wrapped up his days as a diplomat. This is the same chap who took a spear through his jaw and kept on going while trying to find the source of the Nile. The same fellow who traveled undercover to Mecca during the Haj, risking certain death if he'd been caught.

Explorer, ethnographer, undercover spy and author, Burton's exploits as a sex addict were so excruciatingly frank that his widow made a bonfire of his notes upon his death, depriving the world of priceless accounts of life among the Hindus, Muslims, American Indians and much more.

Trieste is a pleasant city by the sea, seeming even more so after lunch by the Grand Canal where a squadron of kayakers are playing water polo. I note that many of the very sexy women of Trieste wear their pants so tight that they appear to be painted on, swaying down the piazzas on tall spike heels - very distracting.

Sir Richard Burton would certainly approve.

If there's one place in all the world that every traveler must visit, it's Italy, with a close second being Thailand. In the weeks ahead, we do northern Italy's greatest hits, with most destinations not more than an hour or two apart by train.

Jeannette and I get totally lost in Venice, which is swarming shoulder-to-snout with tourists. It's like visiting Disneyworld on the busiest day of the year.

"It's nothing like I remember from when we were here before," says Jeannette, sorrowfully, dismayed by the change from the soulful Venice we enjoyed on our honeymoon in 1996.

It seems like half a million people are jammed into the narrow passageways of the town, which are crammed to the gills with souvenir kiosks selling Italian soccer jerseys, masks and plastic trash. The endless souvenir stands are so distracting that you barely notice the ornate buildings and network of canals. We've managed to arrive on May 1, Europe's version of Labor Day.

"How do you get lost in Venice?" I wonder as we're driven from plaza to plaza by the crowds.

"It's a maze," Jeannette says. "It's a-mazing."

We get in a fight with a seafood vendor who insists that deep-fried octopus is "fish." Then we manage to find every wrong turn in the City of Bridges, Bride of the Sea, Queen of the Adriatic, until I'm swearing a blue streak in bewilderment, wound up over the threat of missing our train.

Moving on to Milano, we wander around the capital of fashion in a downpour, marveling at the intricacy of the sculpture on its cathedral walls and the nearby Galleria. This vast clamshell is a glass-covered shopping arcade built in the late 1800s - a temple to fashion buzzing like a hive with thousands of shoppers.

Self-conciously stylish, the streets of Milan are filled with sharp-dressed men decked out in cream-colored slacks, scarves and alligator-hide loafers. Dressy women float by in get-ups that are as rich with frills as fancy desserts. The store windows offer a fashion zoo of precious high-heeled shoes adorned with golden spikes, petals, faux jewels and butterflies. Close behind are herds of excruciatingly expensive handbags bedecked with brass plates and enough cargo space to pack in a baby.

We've seen so many handbags piled up in store windows, kiosks, and peddled by street vendors in every town around the world that they must outnumber the human race itself.

"Why do women need so many handbags?"

"To go with their shoes, obviously," Jeannette says.

In Lago di Como, we hike around town for hours under the weight of our packs, looking in vain for a room.

"None of these hotels seem to be on our map," I say as we slog up and down the streets of this lakeside city. Eventually, we blunder upon a pension's small sign, no bigger than half a license plate, with the place buried in an obscure alley. Amazingly, a room is freshly available, proof once again that Fortune loves its traveling fools.

A blend of Kauai and Switzerland, Lake Como was beloved by the Romance poets of the early 1800s who knocked themselves silly trying to describe the place, emptying the cupboard of adjectives. Suffice to say that here lies a long, thin finger of a lake which wanders for miles under the gaze of misty Alps swaddled in clouds. Ferries run up and down the lake past villages lined with cobblestone streets. High up the mountains are the villas of the very rich - movie stars and old-money royalty - and down on the shore are rows of palazzos, ancient homes and palatial Italianate hotels of the $500 per night variety. The hills are checkered with stone block houses in hues of salmon and cream.

Film star George Clooney hangs his hat in this town, but somehow we manage to miss him over espresso the next morning.

It was in and around this area that Ernest Hemingway set his novel, *A Farewell to Arms*. Set in northern Italy in World War I (spoiler alert!), the novel is about a wounded ambulance driver, Frederic Henry (young Ernie?), who falls for an English nurse, Catherine Barkley. Hemingway employed the ever-dependable convention of literature where the likable protagonist dies at the end of the story. In this case, Catherine's baby is born dead in the wake of a Cesarean section and Catherine dies soon afterward as Frederic walks back to his hotel in the rain.

Literature, it seems, is not that hard to master. Write a slow-moving, minimalist tale where nothing much happens except a great deal of talking embellished with grim details; toss in some three-dollar words like "lyrical" and "euphonious" and kill off your best characters at the end. *Voila*, literature.

Cinque Terre

"Last night I dreamed I was in a gun battle on Union Street back home," I tell Jeannette. "I'm having more anxiety dreams the closer we get to going home because of all of the things that need fixing once we get back. The taxes, the tree that fell through the roof..."

Yes, during a freak storm back home, a pine tree snapped and plunged like a 30-foot spear through the roof of our garage. It's too dangerous for friends and family to handle; it will have to wait until we return to hire a construction crew.

But the tide of anticipating home is growing so deep that sometimes it's hard to focus on Italy. Focus, focus!

One of the excursions we've looked forward to for months is the hike along the Cinque Terre pathway, an old goat path between five villages perched along the cliffs of the Italian Riviera, overlooking the Mediterranean.

"We'll just take daypacks and hike for a few days between the villages," I tell Jeannette. "Just like Ernest Hemingway."

So what a disappointment to find that the Cinque Terre route takes only a few hours at best, and as for goat paths, nada. The beginning of the hike in Monterosso al Mare is a paved walkway laid with millions of stones, as wide as a bike path and crowded with elderly British tourists. They walk the mile or so to Vernazza with the aid of hiking poles as if on an expedition to Kilamanjaro. The tourists are packed elbow-tight as we exit the train connecting the towns, and we can't imagine where they've all come from, since there's not a tourist to be found in the working-class city of Spezia where we're holed up.

Fortunately, Jeannette and I manage to wander "off the beaten path" to a trail high up the cliffs through vineyards perched 1,000 feet about the sea. It's no goat path - perhaps there hasn't been a goat up here in 30 years - but it will do, and we are rewarded near the end of our hike with the Italian version of a lemonade stand. Alongside the trail an elderly farmer is selling shots of limoncello, the Italian lemon liqueur.

Taking on Tuscany

Italy's adventures are as closely packed as its cities. We walk ourselves blue over a couple of days in Firenze (Florence) which offers a maze of streets pouring into a succession of piazzas.

But two days in Firenze have us stuffed to the gills with medieval and Renaissance art and $75 poorer in museum fees. The city's many museums are packed with sculptures and paintings collected or commissioned by the Medici family that ruled Firenze for generations. Greek gods and busts of caesars abound. But as is the case with art museums all over the world, we find them stuffed with depressing religious art from the Middle Ages. Gloomy scenes of crucifixions, martyrs and the Madonna and child stuff that haunts Europe in thousands of paintings, along with the usual naked fat lady depictions of Venus and other gods.

"When you see all of this religious art, you understand why the people of old Europe were so busy murdering and massacring each other for hundreds of years over their differences in dogma," I say as we rest on a street corner. "They couldn't get this shit out of their heads, and I mean for hundreds of years."

"Well, we're more interested in people-watching anyway," Jeannette says, surveying the passing scene of short ones, tall ones, skinny ones and small ones in the Piazza della Signoria.

"It's true, once you've seen a few cathedrals or old art museums, you've seen them all."

"I'd rather walk around the streets than hang out indoors anyway," she says. "You see more."

After seven months on the road, a bit of travel fatigue is starting to set in.

"Forget that idea I had about traveling for the rest of our lives," I say, rubbing the aching soles of my feet. "You can only hang out in public squares, eat in bad restaurants and pee in grimy public toilets for so long before you start feeling a bit rough around the edges. Maybe that's why rock bands trash their rooms."

"I haven't trashed a single room yet," Jeannette notes.

"Very considerate of you."

The 17-foot-tall statue of Michelangelo's David is worth the lengthy wait. But for us, more enthralling than Italy's Renaissance art, is rummaging for bike jerseys in its flea markets. The jerseys are cast-offs from cycle racers who have more than they can manage to pack into their drawers. Back home, cycle jerseys run $80-$120, yet here they're in heaps for as little as $4.

Moving on, we have a moonlight meal at an outdoor café beneath the Leaning Tower of Pisa, a romantic Lady and the Tramp moment in old Italy.

Construction of the tower began In the 1100s, yet when the base was only 30 feet high the earth sank, tilting the tower by six inches. The architect fled town, fearing for his head. It took nearly 200 years to finish the tower in a succession of builders. The tower has been a fixer-upper ever since, and on into the foreseeable future to boot. Still, it's a beautiful wedding cake structure of white marble and a fine adornment for dinner by moonlight.

Pisa has other such marvels but falls short on one score.

"Isn't it odd that the pizza in Pisa is the worst ever?" I say at a snack stop during our hike around the haunts of native son Galileo. "It's like something you'd get wrapped in cellophane that's been microwaved in a gas station. Cardboard."

"You're paying for the atmosphere," Jeannette says. "Maybe the pizza will be better in Rome."

Foodstuffs

Spaghetti and pizza seem to be the staples of every meal in Italy, and though it's hard to imagine, we're getting a bit tired of them. Nor have we had much luck with the famed Tuscan cuisine, the high point of which has been some shreds of greasy, alleged boar meat on a bare plate of pasta. This was accompanied by a handful of boiled, unseasoned white beans, whose flavor is apparently so delicate that we can't even detect it. We also spot a beef dish that runs $35 for a (very) thin sliver of meat. For all we know, it's horse.

Last night we had a pork roast with some gelatinous bean and veggie soup. "My Mom's pork roast was much better, and as for the soup, blah!" I complain.

"Everyone always says their mom's cooking is better," Jeannette says dryly.

I also have the misfortune to order a salsiccia sandwich, which looks good until Jeannette offers her diagnosis. "I think that's fried Spam," she says.

More blah.

Tonight, roast turkey; it's okay, but no better than the average Thanksgiving bird back home, and we've been prepared to expect culinary miracles from world-famous Tuscany.

"If you have the money to go to the hoity-toity places, you'd probably get a feast fit for a Medici duke," I say after our third or fourth bad meal.

"But we're judging the food on what they serve the tourists," Jeannette says. "No wonder it's just so-so."

"I'll bet that all of the rah-rah stuff you read about the cuisine of Tuscany is just BS to sell the memoirs of American foodie authors."

"Yes, but we have to keep trying," Jeannette says. "We can't give in to McDonald's."

Ah, but the gourmand in me finds solace in a small pizza shop, where man-sized hunks of pizza topped with scalloped potatoes and ham prove irresistible. Try as I might, I can't resist another slab every time we pass the place.

And Italy redeems itself with the wine spritzers everyone seems to be sipping in the outdoor cafes at the end of each day: a mix of white wine and Campari, garnished with a slice of orange. *Bellissimo*!

Saddle Up

The high point of our travels through Italy, literally, is a a self-guided week on bicycles through the backroads of Tuscany and over the mountains to Umbria.

Renting bikes, saddle bags and a map from an outfit called Iron Donkey, which is curiously headquartered in Northern Ireland, we roll down the cobblestones of Siena for a week in the Tuscan countryside. We have only a single change of clothes and our toothbrushes to last the week.

All day we ride in the blazing sun past miles of vineyards and rows of cypress trees along with the occasional castle or chapel, riding across hills and valleys that range from 800 to 1,600 feet. Each night we claw our way to the top of some hill town, Montepulciano, Monte San Savino and the like, for views of 30 miles of the Tuscan countryside.

Today we awaken beneath the heavy beams of our room in Montalcino at a hotel constructed in the 1800s.

"It feels like I'm having a total Hemingway-in-Italy experience," I tell Jeannette, lying beside me in bed. Surely, she must be Papa's Italian bimbo.

"Including the wine," she says.

"And the woman."

"Wine, woman and song."

"So hard to resist," I agree. Like Australia, Italy is a wine-lover's wonderland, with the difference being that a bottle of good Italian wine tends to cost less than a 12 oz. can of Coca-Cola.

Sweat pours from our bodies as we climb for miles uphill at the end of each day. Many of Tuscany's towns were built high on hills as a defense against invading barbarian raiders.

"See any barbarians approaching?" I ask as we walk the perimeter of a fortress overlooking miles of farmland.

"Just a big one on a bike," Jeannette says, exhausted from our climb.

"Gee, I sure smell bad," she says a day later after a particularly tough climb into Monte San Savino.

"That's not you. You're walking past a cheese shop."

Eternal Tuscany

Nothing much ever happens in Monte San Savino, and that also seems to be the case for Tuscany in general. Tuscany is a strange, sleepy, dreamy place where it feels like nothing has changed in centuries. The fascists and the Nazis came and went in the 1940s, followed by today's horde of wine-tasting tourists, but the last time anything big happened here was from the 1100s to the 1400s when these hill towns were built from blocks of stone.

Beyond that time, you have to look back to the Romans who ruled here 2,000 years ago and the Etruscans who lived in these hills 1,000 years before them. No one has much of a clue about the Etruscans, except that they established a number of the towns we're staying in and had a civilization of 11 warring city-states. All were built atop high hills and surrounded by walls of 20 feet or more to defend against brigands, invaders and each other.

It's not hard to imagine that this countryside hasn't changed much in centuries: the same rows of cypress trees line the quiet lanes; the same stone houses still perch on the hills above the vineyards. Narrow passageways wind like wormholes through medieval towns without any sense of urban planning and the block towers watch over the valleys as they have for 1,000 years. Eternal Tuscany.

But Tuscany has a beauty to rival heaven, especially if you're pedaling slowly through its countryside on a bike. Last night we sat on a brick wall beneath a watchful pigeon, perched above us in a flowering tree, and witnessed the sun sinking bright as a poppy over the misty hills. Afterward, we ate a rotisserie chicken from a nearby supermarket with our fingers on the rose-draped verandah of our hotel room, washing it down with a *bottiglio* of Chianti.

"This is like the Garden of Eden," Jeannette says. I couldn't agree more.

The Road to Umbria

It's not all easy spinning in the sun, however. On the penultimate day of our ride, severe winds hit us head-on, strong enough to force us to walk a mile or two across a broad field to keep from being thrown off our bikes. We make the long, long climb up to the hill town of Cortona, whipped and burned by whirling winds but happy to have missed the rain.

Said to be older than Troy, Cortona is the town featured in the film, *Under the Tuscan Sun*, and was one of the most important cities in the Etruscan civilization, established more than 2,900 years ago.

The next morning takes us even higher over the mountains dividing Tuscany and Umbria. Up, up, up we ride to around 2,700 feet. It's so cold it could snow, yet we're soaking with sweat by the time we reach the top. But the worst is going downhill when our fingers turn to ice, the cold shooting up to our elbows. We stop several times to warm up on the road winding down the mountains, which ends up being a narrow trail through the forest, passing through villages so quiet they might be ghost towns. One town still has a sign posted on the side of an ancient building, blasting the rule of Il Duce, Mussolini. It's a relic of partisan fighters who fought Italy's fascist government in the '40s.

We ride for miles on a gravel bike trail along the Tiber, which is just a stream here, but swells into a major river by the time it reaches Roma. Toward nightfall, we roll into Sansepolcro in Umbria, taking seven hours to cover 70k. And at last, we have the Tuscan meal we've longed for, albeit in neighboring Umbria: roast beef in peppercorns and rosemary, pasta with duck sauce, fried potatoes, salad and Chianti.

Our celebration is joyful but heavy with the knowledge that in less than a week we'll be homeward bound after 200 days around the world.

Homeward Bound

Rome is one of those towns like New York, London or Paris where you need to spend at least five days to soak up the vibes. We find a windowless room at the oddly named Texas Hotel, enduring a shared, cold-water bathroom that has a shower tighter than a broom closet. But the place is cheap with a great location, and includes a ride in a World War I-era cage elevator.

For the 100th time we walk ourselves dizzy, visiting all of the sights: the Forum, Coliseum, the Pantheon, Font di Trevi, the great piazzas filled with artists and street musicians...

This includes joining 20,000 tourists who squeeze through the halls of the Vatican each day.

"It's a wonder there's any oxygen in here, there are so many people," Jeannette says as we crane our necks backwards for a view of Michelangelo's murals in the Sistine Chapel. We're shoulder-to-shoulder with a vast crowd, slowly digested through the Vatican's gullet.

It's a bit of a thrill to see an actual pope at the Vatican, however, even though this one is Pope John XXIII, who is lying under glass in a crystal coffin in St. Peter's Cathedral. Got to admit, he looks pretty dead.

My very Catholic Aunt Lillian saw PJ 23 on her trip to Europe in the early '60s and it was the thrill of a lifetime for her to attend his weekly papal audience. He died in 1963, soon after her trip, and his remains were put on display for Vatican tourists. Oops, I mean for purposes of veneration.

The exhibition of dead saints and church officials is a religious tradition around the world, but is especially beloved by Catholics. In Siena, we saw crystal reliquaries containing the blackened skulls, jawbones, fingers and other body parts of departed holy men.

Seeing the wan husk of the dead pope made me think of Aunt Lillian again, a very kind and generous person. As is our custom when visiting a church, we light candles in her memory, and for other loved ones who've gone before us.

St Peters Cathedral is fabulous beyond description with its towering sculptures, domes and archways. A truckload of adjectives wouldn't do it justice. It was conceived as the largest cathedral in the world, with a papal injunction against any Catholics daring to build anything bigger.

At the heart of St. Peters we hear tales of the early Christians, who were made scapegoats for the fire that burned down two-thirds of Rome in 64 AD. St. Peter was crucified upside down by Nero on this very spot, and his tomb lies under the altar.

Later, I mention to our hotel manager that the Vatican made for a grueling visit. "The next time you go, you should drink a bottle of Italian wine," he advises in all sincerity. "People don't believe it, but it gives you energy. That's what we do."

Quo Vadis?

A walk down the Appian Way heading south from Rome seems a fitting way to end the final steps of our trip.

This was the main highway through the Roman Empire, constructed over 2,000 years ago from Rome all the way to southern Italy. The world's first tourists traveled this road: wealthy Romans who made a grand tour of Italy, Egypt, the Middle East and Greece under the protection of the Pax Romana - military outposts which shielded them from pirates, brigands and hostile foreigners.

With our flight to the U.S. looming, Jeannette and I are getting antsy with push-me, pull-me feelings about going home.

"I want to take you someplace special," I say on the last day of our trip. "A place to wrap things up."

And so we find ourselves alone on this ancient stone highway, walking along a stretch that is closed to traffic.

The feet of millions of people have polished the irregular paving stones of the Appian Way, including soldiers, traders, pilgrims, Crusaders and those condemned to die. Hundreds of rebel slaves were crucified along this route after the uprising of Spartacus in 71 BC. Crucifixions were a common sight for those entering or leaving Rome for generations; corpses were nailed on crosses as a warning to behave in Caesar's city.

Here too, apocryphal legend has it that the apostle Peter was fleeing for his life when he met the resurrected Jesus just south of Rome.

"Quo vadis?" he asked, meaning, "Where are you going?" Jesus replied that, "I'm going to Rome to be crucified."

As in again.

Peter was so inspired that he turned back to Rome to continue preaching and was martyred for his efforts. It's a poignant sight to see the obscure corner in the road where this meeting is supposed to have taken place - to imagine two lowly travelers who changed the lives of billions, and to hear the ghostly tramp of those who passed this way.

And now we've joined those millions of travelers through the ages, wrapping up seven months around the world. I compose a silent prayer, thanking God for delivering us safely home through all our adventures, and especially for watching over Jeannette.

"Congratulations," I say. "By tomorrow, you'll be an official circumnavigator of the Earth. One of the few in the history of the human race since the time of Magellan who made it all the way around."

"I don't want to go home," Jeannette says as we walk south, "but our family needs us and it's time to get back."

"Right. And I've got to get back to work," I say. "Dorothy was right, there's no place like home for screwing up a perfectly good trip."

"Oh, stop. Don't you want to see the grandkids?"

Of course, but that homing instinct is much stronger for Jeannette. I reflect that grandmothers, like eagles, always return to their nests each year, no matter how far they fly, because our funny, old grandmas are the heart and soul of every family on Earth. They call the shots, shoulder the loads and broker family deals, all while pretending they're just innocent bystanders. We have to go home, it's our destiny.

"I guess we're at that stage of life when the generations that are above and below us need us more than ever," I say at last. "We're broke, anyway."

"The party's over," Jeannette says. "Maybe we'll do it again someday."

"I don't want to go anywhere for a long, long time after this."

"Really?

"No, really."

"I don't believe that," she says. "You're always planning the next trip before we even start the trip we're on."

"No, seriously. We need to work on just staying home for awhile. Fix up the house and stay put."

"Uh-huh. And what if staying home doesn't work out?"

Despite a vow to be a homebody, I can't help myself.

"A trip around the Pacific Rim would be good," I say cautiously. "That would mean traveling down the length of Mexico and Central America to Ecuador and Peru."

"I thought you were going to stay home."

"For sure, but listen," I say as the phantom trip unfolds in my imagination. "In Chile we'd buy an old car and drive a couple thousand miles all the way to the tip of South America with a stop in Argentina. Then we'd head west across the South Pacific to New Zealand, maybe stop in Fiji or Tahiti on the way, and then head up the west side of Australia. We could see Perth and the coast north of there; I hear that western Australia is like another world with no one for miles around. From there we'd head north to Korea. Who know? Maybe we'd hit

Mongolia too."

"Mmmm, Mongolia. Yaks and yurts," Jeannette says. "And will you be taking me along?"

"Well, sure. Where would I be without you?"

"Where would we be without each other?"

We stop to take a picture on the Appian Way, the final one of us together out in the wide world.

"Do you think we really will do it again?" Jeannette wonders.

"Well, you never can tell," I say. "You just have to say the magic words, 'next time.'"

The End

The Little Things

Often, it's the little things that make a big difference in the success of a journey. Following are a few tips we've gleaned through the years:

-- Be sure to upload copies of your passports and important numbers to your email account. Include the phone numbers to call if your credit cards get stolen. If all is lost, you can access your information from an internet cafe.

-- Carry small change and bills in a change purse, available for $1 or so at any market overseas. This, so you don't have to flash your whole wad every time you need coins for a bathroom or a beer on the beach.

-- Carry your wallet in your front pocket. Keep your thumb on it when passing through crowds. This goes for women too; your purse should hold only lipstick and small change.

-- Pack a nightlight so you don't bust a toe on the bedstead or step on a scorpion when you need to use the bathroom at night.

-- Take a headlamp or flashlight with you when you go out at night in any developing country. Often, these places suffer blackouts.

-- Pick up a cheap sari in the market; it can serve as a blanket, pillow, beach towel, cover-up, or God forbid, a privacy tent if you have an unavoidable impulse to flush your bowels far from a potty.

-- Make two printouts of your passports and all of your airline and hotel itineraries to keep in folders, one for you and one for your partner. Back it all up on your iPad or tablet.

-- Carry some "just in case" $100 bills in your money belt so you don't get stuck without cash in a place that has no ATMs or doesn't accept credit cards. $1,000 should do it on a trip of a month or more.

-- But make sure your money belt is super secure; the best bet is a traditional belt that goes through your belt loops with a long zipper down the backside. Money belts that fit under your clothing have an unfortunate tendency to unsnap and fall off. If you use one, make sure it's tucked into your underpants.

-- Avoid credit cards - they are prone to I.D.theft anywhere you go, including the U.S. Plus, cash is king in most developing countries. But if you can't resist, be sure to call your bank and let them know your itinerary in advance so they don't lock your card if you're in some far-off place, like Katmandu.

-- Never carry all of your credit and debit cards in one place. Put one in your passport pouch, one in your toilet kit, etc.

-- You know that travelers checks are as outdated as pay phones, right? ATMs are the way to go nowadays, but only if they are in an obviously secure location, such as a bank or hotel lobby where they're free of tampering.

-- Don't forget: **duct tape** and **bungi cords** (for when your pack breaks), a spare set of **glasses** for when a wave washes your specks off your face, a **first aid kit, universal current converter** and a **corkscrew.**

-- Most important: Smile often and exercise your sense of humor. You want people in foreign countries to like you, right? A smile and a laugh will do more to defuse a tricky situation than all of the tough guy stuff you learned on TV.

Questions for book club readers

Would it be difficult for you to travel with your spouse, sharing virtually every minute for months on end, or would it be a dream come true?

What countries are on your 'bucket list' to visit?

What countries in "Travels With My Wife" did you find least desirable to visit? Most desirable?

What's the longest trip that you've ever taken? Would it be difficult for you to travel for six months or more?

Jeannette Wildman said she took fewer clothes on her seven month trip around the world than she would on a typical weekend to Chicago. Would it be difficult for you to travel for months on end with a bare minimum of clothing?

What would it take for you to achieve your own trip around the world?

Could you travel on a shoestring as the authors did, staying in hostels and cheap guest houses for as little as $10 per night?

The authors make the claim that overseas travel has never been easier and that most countries are safe to visit and are brimming with tourists. Are you afraid to travel to other countries?

Do you agree with author Robert Downes that Americans have a warped view of the world due to fear mongering in the media, i.e., movies, TV, the evening news, etc.?

Do you agree with Downes that a commitment to saving money on a regular basis is the best way to finance an extended trip? How do you save for your vacations?

The authors claim that the best way to see Australia is by camping, both to savor the experience of being "Down Under" and to cut costs. Could you see yourself camping for several months?

Are you more, or less, daring as a traveler today than you were when you were young? What was your biggest adventure during your college years?

Would you feel comfortable riding a camel? One hump or two?

Other books by Robert Downes
from The Wandering Press:

Planet Backpacker (2008) chronicles a five-month solo trip around the world. Packing all of his gear and a half-sized guitar on an old mountain bike, the author cycled the west coast of Ireland, across England and down the Danube. Ditching the bike in Prague, he backpacked on through East Europe, Egypt, India and Southeast Asia.

Packed with laughs, myths, history and memorable characters, *Planet Backpacker* offers advice on how to plan your own trip around the world. $13.95

Biking Northern Michigan: The Best & Safest Routes in the Lower Peninsula (2014) offers more than 35 cycling routes covering 1,065 miles through the top end of the lower peninsula.

The guide includes bike paths, quiet roads and information on dining spots, local history, nightlife options and "must visit" destinations. Also, advice on the best type of bike to ride on specific routes along with essential gear. $13.95

Windigo Moon (coming 2016) A novel of the Anishinaabek, the "True People" of the Ojibwe, beginning in the year 1588 and set in the upper Great Lakes.

Miskomakwa (Red Bear) and Ashagi (Blue Heron) grapple with a historical time of crisis, beset by warring tribes on their borders, the onset of the Little Ice Age of the 1600s and a plague of horrific diseases sweeping the continent brought on by "shadow men" from across the sea. This, amid the threat of a jealous rival, Nika (Lone Goose), who summons the horror known as the windigo.

Windigo Moon celebrates the traditions and myths of the Ojibwe people, before the invasion of white Europeans, offering insights on how they survived and thrived in a harsh environment.

For signed copies by the author visit www.planetbackpacker.net

About the Authors

Jeannette Wildman graduated with a degree in child development from Central Michigan University and ran a home day care over the course of 30 years. An expert gardener, she enjoys yoga, cycling and other fitness pursuits in addition to sharing time with her six grandchildren.

Robert Downes is a journalism graduate of Wayne State University. He co-founded and edited the *Northern Express Weekly* from 1991-2014 in Traverse City, Michigan. A former triathlete and two-time Ironman distance competitor, Downes has visited more than 70 countries, territories and city states. He is also a songwriter and guitarist with the group, Acoustic Dynamite.